A Safety Ma

Ian Hay

Alpha Editions

This edition published in 2023

ISBN : 9789357726450

Design and Setting By
Alpha Editions
www.alphaedis.com
Email - info@alphaedis.com

Contents

BOOK ONE.

THE STRIKING OF THE MATCH.

CHAPTER ONE.

HAPPY FAMILIES.

"Nicky, please, have you got Mr Pots the Painter?"

"No, Stiffy, but I'll trouble you for Mrs Bones the Butcher's Wife. *Thank* you. And Daph, have you got Master Bones the Butcher's Son? *Thank* you. Family! One to me!"

And Nicky, triumphantly plucking from her hand four pink-backed cards, slaps them down upon the table face upwards. They are apparently family portraits. The first—that of Bones *père*—depicts a smug gentleman, with appropriate mutton-chop whiskers, mutilating a fearsome joint upon a block; the second, Mrs Bones, an ample matron in apple-green, proffering to an unseen customer a haunch of what looks like anæmic cab-horse; the third, Miss Bones, engaged in extracting nourishment from a colossal bone shaped like a dumb-bell; the fourth, Master Bones (bearing a strong family likeness to his papa), creeping unwillingly upon an errand, clad in canary trousers and a blue jacket, with a sirloin of beef nestling against his right ear.

It was Saturday night at the Rectory, and the Vereker family—"those absurdly handsome Rectory children," as old Lady Curlew, of Hainings, invariably called them—sat round the dining-room table playing "Happy Families." The rules which govern this absorbing pastime are simple. The families are indeed happy. They contain no widows and no orphans, and each pair of parents possesses one son and one daughter—perhaps the perfect number, for the sides of the house are equally balanced both for purposes of companionship and in the event of sex-warfare. As for procedure, cards are dealt round, and each player endeavours, by requests based upon observation and deduction, to reunite within his own hand the members of an entire family,—an enterprise which, while it fosters in those who undertake it a reverence for the unities of home life, offers a more material and immediate reward in the shape of one point for each family collected. We will look over the shoulders of the players as they sit, and a brief consideration of each hand and of the tactics of its owner will possibly give us the key to the respective dispositions of the Vereker family, as well as a useful lesson in the art of acquiring that priceless possession, a Happy Family.

Before starting on our tour of the table we may note that one member of the company is otherwise engaged. This is Master Anthony Cuthbert Vereker, aged ten years—usually known as Tony. He is the youngest member of the family, and is one of those fortunate people who are never bored, and who rarely require either company or assistance in their amusements. He lives in a world of his own, peopled by folk of his own creation; and with the help of this unseen host, which he can multiply to an indefinite extent and transform into anything he pleases, he organises and carries out schemes of recreation beside which all the Happy Families in the world become humdrum and suburban in tone. He has just taken his seat upon a chair opposite to another chair, across the arms of which he has laid the lid of his big box of bricks, and is feeling in his pocket for an imaginary key, for he is about to give an organ recital in the Albert Hall (which he has never seen) in a style modelled upon that of the village organist, whom he studies through a chink in a curtain every Sunday.

Presently the lid is turned back, and the keyboard—a three-manual affair, ingeniously composed of tiers of wooden bricks—is exposed to view. The organist arranges unseen music and pulls out invisible stops. Then, having risen to set up on the mantelpiece hard by a square of cardboard bearing the figure 1, he resumes his seat, and embarks upon a rendering of Handel's "Largo in G," which its composer, to be just, would have experienced no difficulty in recognising, though he might have expressed some surprise that so large an instrument as the Albert Hall organ should produce so small a volume of sound. But then Handel never played his own Largo in a room full of elder brothers and sisters, immersed in the acquisition of Happy Families and impatient of distracting noises.

The Largo completed, its executant rises to his feet and bows again and again in the direction of the sideboard; and then (the applause apparently having subsided) solemnly turns round the cardboard square on the mantelpiece so as to display the figure 2, and sets to work upon "The Lost Chord."

Meanwhile the Happy Families are being rapidly united. The houses of Pots the Painter, Bun the Baker, and Dose the Doctor lie neatly piled at Nicky's right hand; and that Machiavellian damosel is now engaged in a businesslike quest for the only outstanding member of the family of Grits the Grocer.

Nicky—or Veronica Elizabeth Vereker—was in many respects the most remarkable of the Rectory children. She was thirteen years old, was the only dark-haired member of the family, and (as she was fond of explaining) was possessed of a devil. This remarkable attribute was sometimes adduced as a distinction and sometimes as an excuse,—the former when impressionable and nervous children came to tea, the latter when all other palliatives of crime had failed. Certainly she could lay claim to the brooding spirit, the entire absence of fear, the unlimited low cunning, and the love of sin for its own sake which go to make the master-criminal. At present she was enjoying herself in characteristic fashion. Her brother Stephen—known as "Stiffy"—Nicky's senior by one year, a transparently honest but somewhat limited youth, had for the greater part of the game been applying a slow-moving intellect to the acquisition of one complete Family. Higher he did not look. Nicky's habit was to allow Stiffy, with infinite labour, to collect the majority of the members of a Family in which she herself was interested, and then, at the eleventh hour, to swoop down and strip her unconscious collaborator of his hardly-earned collection.

Stiffy, sighing patiently, had just surrendered Mr, Mrs, and Miss Block (Hairdressers and Dealers in Toilet Requisites) to the depredatory hands of Nicky, and was debating in his mind whether he should endeavour when his next chance came to complete the genealogical tree of Mr Soot the Sweep or corner the clan of Bung the Brewer. Possessing two Bungs to one Soot, he decided on the latter alternative.

Presently he was asked by his elder sister, Cilly (Monica Cecilia), for a card which he did not possess, and this gave him the desired opening.

"I say, Nicky," he began deferentially, "have you got Master Bung?"

Nicky surveyed her hand for a moment, and then raised a pair of liquid-blue eyes and smiled seraphically.

"No, Stiffy, dear," she replied; "but I'll have Mr Bung and Mrs Bung."

Stiffy, resigned as ever, handed over the cards. Suddenly Sebastian Aloysius Vereker, the eldest son of the family (usually addressed as "Ally"), put down his cards and remarked, slowly and without heat—

"Cheating again! My word, Nicky, you are the absolute *edge*!"

"*Who* is cheating?" inquired Veronica in a shocked voice.

"You. Either you *must* have Master Bung, or else you are asking for Stiffy's cards without having any Bungs at all; because I've got Miss myself."

He laid the corybantic young lady in question upon the table to substantiate his statement.

Nicky remained entirely unruffled.

"Oh—*Bung*!" she exclaimed. "Sorry! I thought you said 'Bun,' Stiffy. You should spit out your G's a bit more, my lad. *Bung-gah*—like that! I really must speak to dad about your articulation."

In polite card-playing circles a lady's word is usually accepted as sufficient; but the ordinary courtesies of everyday life do not prevail in a family of six.

"Rot!" said Ally.

"Cheat!" said Cilly.

"Never mind!" said loyal and peaceable Stiffy. "I don't care, really. Let's go on."

"It's not fair," cried Cilly. "Poor Stiffy hasn't got a single Family yet. Give it to him, Nicky, you little beast! Daph, make her!"

Daphne was the eldest of the flock, and for want of a mother dispensed justice and equity to the rest of the family from the heights of nineteen. For the moment she was assisting the organist, who had inadvertently capsized a portion of his keyboard. Now she returned to the table.

"What is it, rabble?" she inquired maternally.

A full-throated chorus informed her, and the arbitress detached the threads of the dispute with effortless dexterity.

"You said you thought he was asking for Miss Bun and not Bung?" she remarked to the accused.

"Yes—that was all," began Nicky. "You see," she continued pathetically, "they're all so beastly unjust to me, and—"

Daphne picked up her small sister's pile of completed Families and turned them over.

"You couldn't have thought Stiffy wanted *Buns*," she said in measured tones, "because they're here. You collected them yourself. You've cheated again. Upstairs, and no jam till Wednesday!"

It is a tribute to Miss Vereker's disciplinary methods that the turbulent Nicky rose at once to her feet and, with a half-tearful, half-defiant reference to her Satanic inhabitant, left the room and departed upstairs, there to meditate on a Bun-strewn past and a jamless future.

Daphne Vereker was perhaps the most beautiful of an extraordinarily attractive family. Her full name was Daphne Margaret. Her parents, whether from inherent piety or on the *lucus a non lucendo* principle, had endowed their offspring with the names of early saints and martyrs. The pagan derivative Daphne was an exception. It had been the name of Brian Vereker's young bride, and had been bestowed, uncanonically linked with that of a saint of blameless antecedents, upon the first baby which had arrived at the Rectory. Mrs Vereker had died eleven years later, two hours after the birth of that fertile genius Anthony Cuthbert, and Brian Vereker, left to wrestle with the upbringing of six children on an insufficient stipend in a remote country parish, had come to lean more and more, in the instinctive but exacting fashion of lonely man, upon the slim shoulders of his eldest daughter.

There are certain attributes of woman before which the male sex, whose sole knowledge of the ways of life is derived from that stern instructor Experience, can only stand and gape in reverent awe. When her mother died Daphne Vereker was a tow-headed, long-legged, irresponsible marauder of eleven. In six months she looked like a rather prim little nursery-governess: in two years she could have taken the chair at a Mother's meeting. Circumstance is a great forcing-house, especially where women are concerned. Her dreamy, unpractical, affectionate father, oblivious of the expectant presence in the offing of numerous female relatives-in-law, had remarked in sober earnest to his little daughter, walking erect by his side in her short black frock on the way home from the funeral:—"You and I will have to bring up the children between us now, Daphne;" and the child, with an odd thrill of pride at being thus promoted to woman's highest office at the age of eleven, had responded with the utmost gravity—

"You had better stick to the parish, dad, and I'll manage the kids."

And she had done it. As she presides at the table this Saturday evening, with her round chin resting on her hands, surveying the picturesque crew of ragamuffins before her, we cannot but congratulate her on the success of her methods, whatever those may be. On her right lolls the apple of her eye, the eldest son, Ally. He is a handsome boy, with a ready smile and a rather weak mouth. He is being educated—God knows by what anxious economies in other directions—at a great public school. When he leaves, which will be shortly, the money will go to educate Stiffy, who is rising fourteen.

Next to Ally sprawls Cilly, an amorphous schoolgirl with long rippling hair and great grey eyes that are alternately full of shy inquiry and hoydenish exuberance. Then comes the chair recently vacated by the Madonna-like Nicky; then the ruddy countenance and cheerful presence of the sunny-tempered Stiffy, completing the circle. In the corner Master Anthony Cuthbert, cherubic and rapturous, is engaged, with every finger and toe in action, upon the final frenzy of the "Hallelujah Chorus." The number 6 stands upon the mantelpiece, for the recital is drawing to a close.

To describe Daphne herself is not easy. One fact is obvious, and that is that she possesses an instinct for dress not as yet acquired by any of her brothers and sisters. Her hair is of a peculiarly radiant gold, reflecting high lights at every turn of her head. Her eyes are brown, of the hue of a Highland burn on a sunny afternoon, and her eyebrows are very level and serene. Her colouring is perfect, and when she smiles we understand why it is that her unregenerate brothers and sisters occasionally address her as "Odol." When her face is in repose—which, to be frank, is not often—there is a pathetic droop at the corners of her mouth, which is perhaps accounted for by the cares of premature responsibility. She is dressed in brown velvet, with a lace collar—evening dress does not prevail in a household which affects high tea, but Daphne always puts on her Sunday frock on Saturday evenings—and, having discovered that certain colours suit her better than others, she has threaded a pale blue ribbon through her hair.

Altogether she is a rather astonishing young person to find sitting contentedly resting her elbows upon a dingy tablecloth in an untidy dining-room which smells of American leather and fried eggs. It is as if one had discovered the Venus de Milo presiding at a Dorcas Society or Helen of Troy serving crumpets in an A.B.C. shop.

The "Hallelujah Chorus" has just stopped dead at that paralysing hiatus of two bars which immediately precedes the final crash, when the door opens and the Reverend Brian Vereker appears. A glance at his clear-cut aristocratic features goes a long way towards deciding the question of the origin of the good looks of "those Rectory children."

He is a tall man—six feet two,—and although he is barely fifty his hair is specklessly white. He looks more like a great prelate or statesman than a country parson. Perhaps he might have been one or the other, had he been born the eldest son of the eldest son of a peer, instead of the youngest son of the youngest. And again, perhaps not. The lines of his face indicate brain rather than character, and after all it is character that brings us out top in this world. There are furrows about his forehead that tell of much study; but about the corners of his mouth, where promptitude and decision usually set their seal, there is nothing—nothing but a smile of rare sweetness. His gentle blue eyes have the dreamy gaze that marks the saints and poets of this world: the steely glitter of the man of action is lacking. Altogether you would say that Brian Vereker would make a noble figurehead to any high enterprise; but you would add that if that enterprise was to succeed, the figurehead would require a good deal of imported driving-power behind it. And you would be right.

The Rector paused in the doorway and surveyed the lamp-lit room.

..."*Halle-lu-u-ja-ah!*" vociferated the Albert Hall organ with an air of triumphant finality. Brian Vereker turned to his youngest son with the ready sympathy of one child for another child's games.

"That's right, Tony! That's the stuff! Good old George Frederick! *He* knew the meaning of the word music—eh?"

"Yes—George Fwederick!" echoed the organist. "*And* Arthur Seymour, daddy! You've just missed 'The Lost Chord.'"

"Ah," said the Rector in a tone of genuine regret, "that's a pity. But we had the Seventy-Eighth Psalm to-night, and I'm later than usual."

"Quadruple chant?" inquired Tony professionally.

"Rather! But is your recital quite over, boyo?"

"Yes—bedtime!" replied the organist, with a reproachful glance in the direction of his eldest sister.

"Run along, dear!" was all the comfort he received from that inflexible despot.

"All right! I must lock up, though."

Master Tony removed the last number from the mantelpiece, disintegrated his keyboard and packed it up with the other bricks, and drawing aside the window-curtain remarked solemnly into the dark recess behind it—

"That will be all to-night, organ-blower. You can go home now."

To which a husky and ventriloquial voice replied—

"Thank you kindly, Mr Handel, sir. Good-night."

"Now," concluded Mr Handel, turning to his elders with the air of a martyr addressing a group of arena lions, "I'm ready!"

"Take him up, Cilly dear," said Daphne. "I must look after dad's supper."

"Come on, Tony," said Cilly, uncoiling her long legs from under her and rising from the hearthrug.

"Righto!" said Tony. "You be a cart-horse and I'll be a broken-down motor."

Monica Cecilia Vereker meekly complied, and departed upstairs, towing the inanimate mechanism of the inventive Anthony behind her bump by bump, utilising her sash, which she had removed for the purpose, as a tow-rope.

"Ally and Stiffy," commanded Daphne, turning to the two remaining members of the family, "you'd better go and pump the cistern full. Saturday night, you know, and the kids' baths have just been filled; so look sharp before the boiler bursts."

Stiffy, obliging as ever, rose at once; Ally, cumbered by that majesty which doth hedge a sixth-form boy and a member of the school Fifteen (especially when ordered about by a female), was more deliberate in his acquiescence. However, presently both the boys were gone, and five minutes later Daphne, with the assistance of the one little maid whom the establishment supported, had laid the Rector's supper. She installed her father in his seat on one side of the table, and took her own on the other, assisting the progress of the meal from time to time, but for the most part sitting with her chin resting upon her two fists, and contemplating the tired man before her with serious brown eyes. Twice she had to leave her seat, once to remove the butter from the vicinity of her parent's elbow, and once to frustrate an attempt on the part of that excellent but absent-minded man to sprinkle sugar over a lettuce.

"Well, my daughter," remarked the Rector presently, "what of the weekly report?"

Saturday night at the Rectory was reserved for a sort of domestic budget.

"Here are the books," said Daphne. "They're much as usual, except that I had to pay two bob on Wednesday for a bottle of embrocation for Ally. He is in training for the mile in the sports at the beginning of next term, and it does his muscles so much good."

"When I won the mile at Fenner's, Daphne," began the Reverend Brian, with a sudden glow of reminiscence in his dreamy eyes, "I did it without embrocation, or any other new-fashioned—"

"Yes, dear, but they have to run so much *faster* now than they did," explained Daphne soothingly. "Then, about the kitchen chimney—"

"But I only took four minutes, twenty-eight—"

"Yes, old man, and I'm *proud* of you!" said Daphne swiftly. "Well, the sweep is coming in on Wednesday, when you'll be away at Wilford, so *that's* all right." She was anxious to get away from the question of the embrocation. It had been a rank extravagance, and she knew it; but Ally was ever her weak spot. "Then, I've got three-and-nine in hand out of current expenses just now, and if I take two half-crowns out of the emergency bag and we go without a second joint this week, I can get Nicky a new pair of boots, if you don't mind. (Don't cut the cheese with a spoon, dear; take this knife.) Of course, we ought not to have to go to the emergency bag for boots at all. It's rather upsetting. To-day I find that a perfectly ducky pair of Sunday shoes, which I outgrew just before I stopped growing, and was keeping specially for that child, are too small for her by yards. (I had tried them on Cilly a year ago, but she simply couldn't get her toe in.) And now they'll be wasted, because there are no more of us girls. My feet are *most* exasperating."

"Your mother had tiny feet," said the Rector, half to himself.

He pushed away his plate, and gazed absently before him into that land where his son Tony still spent so much of his time, and whither Tony's young and pretty mother had been borne away eleven years before. Daphne permitted him a reverie of five minutes, while she puckered her brow over the account-books. Then she rose and took down a pipe from a rack on the mantelpiece. This she filled from a cracked jar thirty years old, adorned with the coat-of-arms of one of the three royal colleges of Cambridge, and laid it by her father's left hand.

"Then there's another thing," she continued, lighting a spill at the fire. "Isn't it time to enter Stiffy for school? Mr Allnutt asked us to say definitely by April whether he was coming to fill Ally's place after summer or not, otherwise he would be obliged to give the vacancy to some one else. It's the end of March now."

The Rector lit his pipe—his one luxury—in a meditative fashion, and then leaned back to contemplate his daughter, with her glinting hair and troubled little frown.

"Mr Allnutt? To be sure! Of course! A ripe scholar, Daphne, and a long-standing personal friend of my own. He took the Porson and Craven in successive years. His Iambics——"

All this was highly irrelevant, and exceedingly characteristic. Daphne waited patiently through a *résumé* of Mr Allnutt's achievements as a scholar and a divine, and continued:—

"Will you enter Stiffy at once, then? It would be a pity not to get him into Ally's old house."

Brian Vereker, suddenly recalled to business, laid down his pipe and sighed.

"Boys are terribly expensive things, little daughter," he said. "And we are so very very poor. I wonder if they are worth it."

"Of *course* they are, the dears!" said Daphne, up in arms at once.

"Of course, of course," agreed the Rector apologetically. "You are right, child; you are always right. It is ungrateful and un-Christian of me to give expression to such thoughts when God has granted me three good sons. Still, I admit it *was* a disappointment to me when Ally failed to gain a scholarship at Cambridge. He may have been right in his assertion that there were an exceptionally strong set of candidates up on that occasion, but it was unfortunate that he should have overslept himself on the morning of the Greek Prose Paper, even though, as he pointed out, Greek Prose is his weak subject. What a pity! Strange lodgings, probably! Still, his disappointment must be far greater than ours, so it would be ungenerous to dwell further on the matter. But I fail to see at present how he can be started in life now. If only one had a little money to spare! I have never felt the need of such a thing before."

"Yes, we could do with a touch of it," assented Miss Vereker elegantly. She began to tick off the family requirements on her fingers. "There's Ally to be started in life; and Cilly ought to be sent somewhere and finished—she's tragically gawky, and she'd be perfectly lovely if she was given half a chance; and Stiffy has to be sent to school; and the two kiddies are growing up, and this house is simply tumbling down for want of repairs; and it's really time you had a curate for long-distance visiting."

"Never!" said Brian Vereker firmly.

"All right. Never, if you like, but he'll have to come some day," said Daphne serenely. (The question of the curate cropped up almost as regularly as that of the second joint on Wednesdays.) "And all we've got to run the whole show on," she concluded, with a pathetic little frown which many a man would gladly have given his whole estate to smooth away, "is—two pounds seventeen and ninepence in the emergency bag! It's a bit thick, isn't it?"

Brian Vereker surveyed his daughter's troubled countenance with characteristic placidity. Simple faith—some called it unpractical optimism—was the main article of his creed.

"The Lord will provide, my daughter," he said.

At this moment the door opened with a flourish, and, the crimson and enraged countenance of Master Anthony Cuthbert Vereker having been thrust into the room, its owner inquired, in a voice rendered husky by indignation, how any one could be expected to impersonate a Dreadnought going into action in the bath, when the said bath was encumbered with the flotsam and jetsam of a previous occupant. In other words, was he to be bathed in the same water as Nicky?

It was an old grievance, arising from the insufficient nature of the Rectory water-supply (which had to be pumped up by hand from the garden) and the smallness of the kitchen boiler; and Daphne had perforce to go upstairs to adjust it. Consequently the sitting of the Committee of Ways and Means, with all its immediate necessities and problems for the future, was incontinently suspended.

CHAPTER TWO.

WANTED, A MAN.

Five gentlemen sat side by side along a baize-covered table in a dingy room in a dingier building not far from the principal pit-head of Mirkley Colliery. They were the representatives of the local Colliery Owners' Association, and they were assembled and met together for the purpose of receiving a deputation representing the united interests and collective wisdom of their *employés*.

It should be noted that although there were five gentlemen present, six chairs were set along the table.

Now a deputation may be defined as an instrument designed to extract from you something which you have not the slightest desire to give up. Consequently the reception of such, whether you be a damsel listening for the rat-a-tat of an undesired suitor who has written asking for an interview, or a dethroned Royal Family sitting in its deserted abode awaiting the irruption of a Committee of Public Safety composed of the greater part of its late loyal subjects armed with billhooks and asking for blood, is always an uncomfortable business at the best. Our five gentlemen do not appear to be enjoying their present position any more than the two examples cited above. In fact, they look so exceedingly averse to interviews or arguments of any description, that we will leave them for a moment and divert our attention to the deputation itself, which is delicately skirting puddles of coal-black water and heaps of pit refuse on its way from the boiler-house, where its members have assembled, to the office-buildings of the colliery.

They are six in number, and we will describe them *seriatim*.

Mr Tom Winch is a professional agitator, though he calls himself something else. He is loud-voiced, and ceaseless in argument of a sort. His notion of a typical member of the upper classes is a debilitated imbecile suffering from chronic alcoholism and various maladies incident on over-indulgence, who divides his time between gloating over money-bags and grinding the faces of the poor. He privately regards Trades Unions as an antiquated drag upon the wheels of that chariot at the tail of which he hopes one day to see Capital led captive, gentlemen like Mr Tom Winch handling the reins and plying the whip.

Mr Amos Entwistle is a working collier, and is rightly regarded by both parties as a safe man. He is habitually sober, scrupulously honest, and has worked at Belton Pit for nearly forty years. He looks upon Trades Unions as his father and mother.

Mr Jacob Entwistle is the Nestor of the party. (Amos is his son.) He is a patriarchal old gentleman, with a long white beard, the manner of an ambassador, the deafness of an adder, and the obstinacy of a mule. Altogether he is just the sort of man to prove a valuable asset to any properly constituted deputation. He is the senior member of the local branch of the *Employés'* Association. He regards himself as the father and mother of Trades Unions.

Mr Albert Brash is an expert in the art of what may be called Righteous Indignation. Never was there such an exploiter of grievances. Is short time declared? Mr Brash calls for an Act of Parliament. Is there an explosion of fire-damp? Mr Brash mutters darkly that one of these days a director must swing. Does a careless worker remove a pit-prop and bring down an avalanche of coal on himself? Mr Brash raises clenched hands to heaven and clamours for a revolution. So persistently and so methodically does Mr Brash lay upon the shoulders of Capital the responsibility for all the ills to which flesh is liable, from a hard winter to triplets, that he has ultimately (as is the way in this short-sighted world of ours) achieved the position of Sir Oracle. His deportment is that of a stage conspirator, and he rarely speaks above a hoarse and arresting whisper. He calls himself an Anarchist, but he quails at the passing of the most benevolent policeman. He regards Trades Unions as well-meaning institutions, with but little discrimination as to their choice of leaders.

Mr James Killick is a thoroughly honest, thoroughly muddle-headed Socialist of a rather common type. Like many a wiser and more observant man before him, he has realised something of the grinding misery and suffering of this world, and a great and vague desire to better things is surging inarticulately within him. He has come to the conclusion, as most half-educated philosophers usually do, that the simplest remedy would be to take from those who have and give the proceeds to those who have not. The fact that the world is divided into men to whose hands money sticks like glue and men through whose fingers it slips like water, and that consequently a Utopian re-distribution of property would have to be repeated at inconveniently frequent intervals in order to preserve the social balance, has not yet been borne in on him. He regards Trades Unionism as a broken reed.

Mr Adam Wilkie is a Scot of the dourest and most sepulchral appearance. Native reticence and an extremely cautious manner of expressing himself have invested him with that halo of business acumen which appears to be inevitable to the Scot as viewed by the Sassenach, and his very silence is regarded with respectful admiration by his more verbose colleagues. In reality, he is an intensely stupid, entirely placid individual. Still, he has kept himself by native thrift in tolerable comfort all his life without extraneous assistance, and he consequently regards Trades Unionism as an institution specially and mercifully introduced by Providence for the purpose of keeping the weak-kneed English out of the poorhouse.

"Who's to be there?" inquired Mr Brash of Mr Entwistle senior.

That patriarch, who was negotiating a mountainous waste-heap, made no reply.

"Who are we going to meet?" repeated Mr Brash in a louder tone.

"Eh?" inquires Mr Entwistle, giving his invariable answer to any sudden question.

"Who are we going to *meet*?" bawled Mr Winch.

Mr Entwistle, who was never at a loss a second time, smiled benignantly and replied—

"Ay, that's so. But maybe we can manage to dry 'em at the fire in the office."

"I expect there will be five of them, Mr Winch," interpolated Amos, coming to the rescue. "Kirkley, Thompson, Crisp, Aymer, Montague——"

There was a grunt of disapproval from Mr Wilkie as the last name was mentioned.

"Yon felly!" he observed darkly. "Aha! Mphm!"

Then he relapsed into silence. It was upon such safe utterances as these that Mr Wilkie's reputation for profound wisdom was based.

"Is that all?" said Winch. "Because if it is, I'll undertake to learn that lot right enough! Kirkley, of course, is just an empty-headed aristocrat: he don't count. Then that Crisp—he's too cautious to do anything. We can talk Thompson round all right: done it half a dozen times meself. Aymer never knows his own mind two minutes together, and Moses is a coward. But *is* that all? Ain't the big man going to be there? He's the lad that counts in that crowd."

"He was away in London yesterday," said Entwistle junior. "But you never know——"

"Wallowing in the vice and luxury of the metropolis!" chanted Mr Brash suddenly, as if from some internal missal. "The master absent, squandering his tainted millions, while we stay here and starve! If I was a Member o' Parliament——"

"Talk sense," said Amos Entwistle curtly. "He may be back for all we know. Anyway, they're certain to bring him up if they can, because they know they can't do without him. Mind that tank-engine, father."

He impelled his aged parent, who, oblivious to delirious whistling, was resolutely obstructing the progress of a diminutive locomotive hauling a string of trucks, on to safer ground.

"Well, we'll hope for the best," said Mr Winch piously. "It would be something if he was to come late, even. Give me twenty minutes with the rest before he can get his oar in, and I'll undertake to make them outvote him."

By this time the deputation had arrived at the managerial offices, and five minutes later they were admitted to the presence of the Board. They did not know that they had been immediately preceded by an orange-coloured envelope, which was eagerly torn open by Lord Kirkley, the deputy-chairman.

"Good egg!" observed his lordship, with a sigh of heartfelt relief. "Juggernaut's coming."

A gentle murmur of satisfaction was audible. Evidently the Board felt the need of a little stiffening. We may as well describe them.

The Marquis of Kirkley was more accustomed to exercising a kindly despotism over rustics who lived contentedly on fourteen shillings a-week than to splitting hairs with unbending mechanics earning four pounds, whose views on the relations between master and man were dictated by a cast-iron bureaucracy, and who regarded not the elastic laws of Give and Take. He was a handsome, breezy, kind-hearted patrician of thirty-four, and considered Trades Unions a damned interfering nuisance.

James Crisp was a solicitor, and represented the Dean and Chapter of Kilchester, beneath the very foundation of whose mighty cathedral ran a very profitable little seam of coal, which was chiefly responsible for making the bishopric of the diocese one of the richest ecclesiastical plums in England. He was a shrewd man of business, probably the best qualified of those present to take the lead in the present instance. Consequently he remained studiously in the background. He regarded Trades Unions as inevitable, but by no means invulnerable.

Sir Nigel Thompson had inherited great possessions, including a colliery, from his father. There was no vice in him, but he loved coal about as much as a schoolboy loves irregular verbs, and his only passions in life were old furniture and chemical research. He attended under compulsion, having torn himself from his comfortable house in London at the bidding of his manager, in whose hands he was reported (not altogether unjustly) to be as wax. He was full of theoretical enthusiasm for Trades Unions, which he identified in some mysterious way with the liberty of the individual; but wished mildly that people could contrive to settle their affairs without dragging him north. Altogether a pleasant but entirely useless member of the Board.

Mr Alfred Aymer was the owner of Cherry Hill Colliery. He was middle-aged, timorous, and precipitate. Left to himself, he would probably have been a kind and fair-dealing employer. But it was his misfortune to be so constituted that his opinions on any subject were invariably those of the last man with whom he had discussed it. Consequently his line of action in the affairs of life was something in the nature of an alternating electric current. After an interview with his manager he would issue a decree of unparalleled ferocity: after five minutes with a deputation of *employés* he would rescind all previous resolutions and promise a perfectly fabulous bonus next pay-day. In his present company he was an adamantine Capitalist, and regarded Trades Unions as the most pernicious of institutions.

Last of all came Mr Montague, whose surname at an earlier and less distinguished period in his history had probably rhymed with "noses." He came from London, where he earned a livelihood by acquiring the controlling interest in various commercial ventures, and making these pay cent per cent. He had recently become proprietor of Marbledown Colliery, and it was said that he was making a better thing out of it than his *employés*. He regarded Trade Unions as an impertinent infringement of the right of the upper classes to keep the lower classes in their proper place. From which the intelligent reader will have no difficulty in deciding to which class Mr Montague considered that he himself belonged.

The deputation was introduced with the usual formalities. Its object was to effect the reinstatement of two *employés* at Marbledown Colliery, an engineman and a hewer, who had been summarily dismissed from their positions for endeavouring, in a society whose relations had never been of the most cordial, to heighten dissension between master and man.

Mr Tom Winch's version of the case, delivered with great wealth of detail and a good deal of unnecessary shouting, was different. The men, it appeared, were models of what enginemen and hewers should be. Their sole offence consisted in having incurred the dislike of the mine-manager, Mr Dodd—whether through their own sturdy independence as true-born Englishmen (*applause from Mr Brash*), or the natural jealousy of an incompetent official towards two able and increasingly prominent subordinates, it was not for Mr Winch to say. Proceeding, the orator warmed to his work, and mentioned that one man was as good as another. Indeed, but for the merest accident of fortune, Lord Kirkley himself might be delving for coal in the bowels of the earth, what time Messrs Conlin and Murton, the dismissed *employés*, sate in the House of Lords smoking cigars and drinking champagne.

After this singularly convincing peroration Mr Winch fell back into line with his companions, amid the *sotto voce* commendations of Messrs Brash and Killick. Mr Aymer, who had been taking notes on a sheet of paper, tore it up with a resigned air of finality. The case was clear: these poor fellows must be reinstated.

The chairman conferred briefly with Mr Crisp.

"Would any other of you gentlemen like to say anything?" he inquired.

The question was communicated to Mr Entwistle senior, who stepped forward and delivered himself of a courtly but rambling discourse, consisting chiefly of reminiscences of something portentous but unintelligible which had happened forty years ago, and even to the most irrelevant mind presented no sort of bearing upon the case whatsoever.

After this Lord Kirkley replied. His remarks were not convincing, for he was hampered in dealing with the question by complete inability to understand where the men's grievance came in, and said so. The owners, he explained, tried to do the fair thing, and most of them did considerably more. Sick funds, pensions, benevolent schemes, and all that sort of thing, didn't they know? He quite admitted that an employer of labour had grave responsibilities and duties laid upon him, and he for one had always tried to live up to them. But hang it! surely an employer had the right to get rid of a couple of fellows who went about preaching anarchy and red revolution in all the public-houses in the district—what? He did not mind ordinary grousing. It did everybody good to blow off steam periodically: he did it himself. But there was grousing and grousing: and when it came to the sort of game that Messrs Conlin and Murton were playing, it was his lordship's opinion that a *ne plus ultra* of thickness had been attained.

The chairman concluded a somewhat colloquial address amid a deathly silence, and the deputation and the board glared uncomfortably at one another. An *impasse* had been reached, it was clear.

"It's all very well, gentlemen," broke in Killick suddenly, "for you aristocrats——"

Lord Kirkley, who was not without a certain sense of proportion, glanced involuntarily at Mr Montague and then at Mr Killick. Did this omniscient and self-opinionated son of toil really see no moral difference between a Peer of the realm, with centuries of clean-bred ancestry behind him, and a man who wore diamond rings and elastic-sided boots? Mr Montague looked up, and regarded Mr Killick with something akin to affection.

There was a sudden rumble underneath the windows, accompanied by the hoot of a motor-horn.

The drama having run itself to a deadlock, the *deus* had duly arrived—in his *machina*.

CHAPTER THREE.

THE WHEELS OF JUGGERNAUT.

There was a dead silence, unbroken until Juggernaut entered the room.

"Good-morning, gentlemen," he said briskly. "I am glad to see that the deputation has only just arrived."

He turned to the clerk who had shown him in.

"Andrews," he said, "bring chairs for these gentlemen, and then we can get to business."

Chairs were brought, and the deputation, which had been balancing itself on alternate legs for nearly half an hour, sat down with an enhanced sense of comfort and importance to what they realised at once was to be the interview proper.

Juggernaut took the seat at the middle of the table vacated by Lord Kirkley, and inquired—

"Has any one spoken yet?"

Progress was reported by Mr Crisp.

"I wonder if I might trouble the deputation again," said the chairman. "Not you, Mr Winch, thank you!" as that Demosthenes cleared his throat in a threatening manner. "In the first place, you don't represent the men in any sense. In fact, considering that you are engaged in no employment in this district, I think it would have been much wiser on the part of those responsible for this deputation to have left you out altogether. You are not even a properly accredited Trades Union official."

"Gentlemen of the Board," began Mr Winch portentously, "I appeal———"

"Don't trouble, really, Mr Winch," broke in Juggernaut with inflexible cheerfulness. "You see, I know exactly what you are going to say. I have heard it so often in other places where you have been kind enough to come forward and champion the cause—of—of—the oppressed millions of this country. That's right, isn't it?"

A muffled sound proceeded from the interior of Mr Wilkie—his first contribution to the debate—and the chairman proceeded.

"I wonder if Mr Entwistle junior would kindly give us the facts."

Amos Entwistle, rising from his seat, re-stated the case of the two men. They were competent and industrious workmen, he maintained, and so long as they gave satisfaction in their situations their private lives and leisure occupations were entirely their own concern. Possibly their views on the relations of Labour and Capital were extreme, but the speaker begged respectfully to point out that there were extremists on both sides; and since many employers might and did regard the men they paid as dirt beneath their feet, it seemed only natural that a section of the men should regard their employers as bullies and tyrants. Mr Entwistle followed up this undoubted home-thrust with a request for a categorical list of the offences alleged against the two men, and solemnly but respectfully warned the Board against risking a serious upheaval by endeavouring to stifle legitimate criticism of its actions. With apologies for plain-speaking he resumed his seat, and Mr Aymer tore up a sheet of paper upon which he had commenced operations on the arrival of the chairman.

"Would any other gentleman like to say anything?" inquired Juggernaut. "Mr Brash? Mr Wilkie?"

No, the gentlemen addressed had nothing to say. Their *forte* was plainly that of chorus.

"Very well," said Juggernaut. "In the first place, I am going to accede to Mr Entwistle's perfectly just request that a definite reason should be given for the dismissal of these men. I agree with him that it is a foolish thing to stifle legitimate criticism. Unfortunately, I don't agree with him that the criticisms of Messrs Conlin and Murton *are* legitimate. I have been making inquiries into the antecedents of these two. Murton is a paid agitator. He is not a local man. He came here less than a year ago, and has been making deliberate mischief ever since. He has money to spend: he backs his arguments with beer. I shouldn't be surprised if he drew his salary from the organisation which retains your services, Mr Winch."

Mr Winch's small eyes began to protrude. He did not relish this line of argument. In dealing with Boards and other representatives of bloated Capital he preferred to keep to the high moral and sentimental plane—the sufferings of the downtrodden sons of Labour, the equality of all men in the sight of God, and so on. Mundane personalities, coupled with the suggestion that he, a high priest of altruism, was making a good thing out of his exertions on behalf of his fellow-toilers, took him below the belt, he considered.

"Conlin," continued Juggernaut, disregarding the fermenting Mr Winch, "seems to be a comparatively sincere and honest grumbler. He has realised that this is an unjust world, and he wants to put it right by Act of Parliament. Consequently he goes about advocating certain special and particular forms of legislation which, if they came into being, would benefit about one member of the community in a hundred and be grossly unfair to the other ninety-nine. He has not yet discovered for himself that the aim of all legislation must be to benefit the type and not the individual. That is the rock upon which all your friends split, Mr Winch. You are always trying to legislate for special cases, and it can't be *done*. I quite agree with you that the conditions of labour in parts of this country are deplorable. We all want to put them right. But there are two things we cannot do. We can't cure them in a hurry, and we can't cure them by swallowing quack medicines. What we have to do is to set to work on systematic lines, and go on working, with patience and a sense of proportion, until our whole social fabric develops into a sounder and more healthy condition. That requires time, and time requires patience, and patience requires common-sense, and common-sense is a thing which is lamentably scarce in this world, Mr Winch. We are marching on to a better state of things every year; but every bit of unsound, panic-stricken, vote-catching legislation—Right-to-Work Bills, Unemployment Acts, and so on—throws us back a step, because its tendency is to remove the symptom instead of curing the disease. Now, symptoms are very valuable assets. They give us reliable and necessary information, which is more than can be said of most intelligence departments. If ever you have such a vulgar thing as a pain in your stomach, Mr Winch, that is a kindly hint from Nature that there is something wrong with the works. If you drink two of whisky hot the pain may cease, but it does not follow that the real cause of the trouble has been removed. In effect you have merely put back the danger-signal to safety without removing the danger. That is just what all this despicable, hand-to-mouth, time-serving legislation that you and your friends are trying to force upon a popularity-hunting Government is doing for the country to-day."

The speaker paused. The deputation wore a distinctly chastened appearance. Mr Aymer was engaged upon a third sheet of notes. Sir Nigel Thompson was working out a chemical formula on the back of an envelope.

"Let us get back to the point, sir," said Amos Entwistle doggedly. "I agree with a great deal of what you say——"

"Shame!" interpolated Mr Killick suddenly.

"But we came here to ask for the reinstatement of these two men, and not to discuss social problems."

"Granted all the time," said Juggernaut cheerfully. "I admit that I have not made Messrs Conlin and Murton my Alpha and Omega in these remarks of mine; but that is because I deliberately went back to first principles instead of cutting into the middle of things. Now for your request! You want an answer? Here it is. The two men cannot be reinstated under any circumstances whatsoever. I confess I am rather sorry for Conlin: he is in a different class from Murton. But he is tarred with the same brush, and he must go."

"Take care, Sir John," broke in Mr Winch, in the declamatory bray which he reserved for extreme crises. "Don't push us too hard! What if a strike was to be proclaimed at Marbledown Colliery? You wouldn't like that, Mr Montague! You have a bad enough name in the district as it is. You grind your 'eel——"

"Mr Winch," said Juggernaut in a voice of thunder, "I must ask you to address yourself to me. This matter has been taken out of Mr Montague's hands by the combined action of the Owners' Association; so if you have any strictures to offer they must be laid upon me as representing the Association collectively. As for striking—well, you struck before, you know. I don't think any of us have forgotten that winter—masters or men!"

"We nearly beat you then," said Killick hotly.

"That," retorted Mr Montague, suddenly breaking into the debate, "was because some sentimental fool sent food and necessaries to your wives."

"It's the women and children who pay for strikes, you know, Mr Winch," said Mr Crisp, speaking for the first time—"not you men. You can do without beer and baccy at a pinch, but your families must have groceries and fire. If they had not been kept going by that unknown benefactor the strike would have collapsed as soon as the Union funds gave out."

"Perhaps they will be kept going again," said Amos Entwistle quietly.

"They won't," said Juggernaut emphatically. "You can take my word for that, Mr Entwistle. I have seen to it. And I may add that if you consider it advisable to proclaim a sectional strike, the owners on their part might find it necessary to declare a lock-out at all the collieries in the district. If men can combine, so can masters."

There was a staggered silence. Even the Board were hardly prepared for this. Juggernaut had so dominated the situation since his arrival that one or two—Mr Montague in particular—were beginning to wonder rather peevishly why they had been admitted to the meeting. But Mr Crisp leaned back and took snuff contentedly. He appreciated strong measures, though he was averse to initiating them.

Still, the temper of the meeting was rising. Killick broke out furiously. It was a burning shame, a monstrous iniquity, he declared, that men who had never done an honest day's work in their lives should be enabled, simply because they had money in their pockets, to force humiliating conditions on a majority who had no alternative but to submit or starve. He spoke with all the conviction that absolute sincerity carries; but the effect of his philippic was not enhanced by the marginal comments of his colleague, Mr Brash, who kept up a running fire of *sotto voce* references to bloody-minded tyrants, champagne, ballet-girls, and other equally relevant topics with a persistence and enthusiasm which would have proved embarrassing to a more self-conscious and less frenzied rhetorician than Mr Killick.

When both solo and *obligato* had subsided, Juggernaut spoke again.

"It is one of the most common delusions of men of your way of thinking, Mr Killick, to imagine that the only kind of work worthy of the name is manual labour. Personally, I have tried both. For two years after I came down from the University I worked for experience's sake in a pit not far from here. I went down with my shift daily and worked full time; but I assure you that those two years were far from being the most laborious of my life."

"Your case was different, sir," said Amos Entwistle, with a practical man's quick perception of his opponent's weak points. "You were doing it for pleasure, to acquire experience—not to earn your bread. You could look forward to something better later on."

"And so can every man!" replied Juggernaut. "Each one of us is able if he likes to work his way up, and up, and up; and the lower he starts, the greater is his range of opportunity. The man at the bottom has the whole ladder to climb, instead of a few paltry rungs, as is the case of a man born near the top. Let him think of that, and be thankful!"

The chairman's sombre eyes glowed. His tone of raillery was gone: he was in sober earnest now. To him poverty and riches were nothing; he could have lived happily on a pound a-week: the salt of life lay in the overcoming of its difficulties.

But Amos Entwistle was a man of tough fibre—by far the strongest man, next to the chairman, in that assemblage.

"You can't deny, sir," he persisted doggedly, "that it is very difficult for a poor man to rise. His employers don't help him much. They are best satisfied with a man who keeps his proper station, as they call it."

"Tyrants!" interpolated Mr Winch hastily.

"Star Chamber!" added Mr Brash, *à propos de bottes.*

"Tyrants? Star Chamber?" Juggernaut surveyed the interrupter quizzically. "Here is a question for you, Mr Brash. Which is the worse—the tyranny of the harsh employer who gathers where he has not strawed, or the tyranny of a Trades Union which a man is forced to join, and which compels the best worker to slow down his pace to that of the worst, and frequently compels him to come out on strike over some question upon which he is perfectly satisfied? I won't attempt to place them in order of merit, but I should feel inclined to bracket—"

"Trades Unions," interrupted Mr Winch, who was beginning to feel himself unduly excluded from the present symposium, "are the first steps towards the complete emancipation of Labour"—he smacked his lips as over a savoury bakemeat—"from the degrading shackles of Capital. Every man his own master!"

Juggernaut nodded his head slowly.

"Ye-es," he said. "That sounds admirable. But what does it *mean* exactly? As far as I can see, it means that every one who is at present a labourer is ultimately going to become a capitalist. In that case it rather looks as if there would be a shortage of hands if there was work to be done. Your Utopia, Mr Winch, appears to me to resemble the Grand Army of Hayti, which consists of five hundred privates and eleven hundred Generals. No, no; you must bear in mind this fact, that ever since the world began mankind has been divided up into masters and men, and will continue to be so divided until the end of time. What we—you and I—have to do is to adjust the relations between the two in such a fashion as to make the conditions fair for both. I don't say that employers aren't frequently most high-handed and tyrannical, but I also say that *employés* are extraordinarily touchy and thin-skinned. I think it chiefly arises from a sort of distorted notion that there is something degrading and undignified in obeying an order. Why, man, obedience and discipline are the very life-blood of every institution worthy of the name. They are no class affair either. I have seen the captain of a company stand at attention without winking for ten minutes, and receive a damning from his colonel that no non-commissioned officer in the service would have dreamed of administering to a private of the line. Master and man each hold equally honourable positions; and what you must drum into the minds of your associates, gentlemen—I'm speaking to the Board as much as to the deputation—is the fact that the interests of both are *identical*, instead of being as far apart as the poles, which appears to be your present impression. Neither can exist without the other. So far you have imbibed only half of that truth. You reiterate with distressing frequency, Mr Winch, the fact that Capital cannot exist without Labour. Perfectly true. Now try to absorb into your system the fact—equally important to a hair's-breadth—that Labour cannot exist without Capital. Each depends upon the other for existence, and what we have to do is to balance and balance and balance, employing a sense of proportion, proportion, *proportion*!"

Juggernaut's fist descended with a crash upon the table, and for a minute he was silent—free-wheeling, so to speak, over the pulverised remains of Mr Winch. Presently he continued, with one of his rare smiles—

"A Frenchman once said that an Englishman begins by making a speech and ends by preaching a sermon. I am afraid I have justified the gibe, but it's a good thing to thrash these matters out. I don't deny that the average employer is in the habit of giving his *employés* their bare pound of flesh in the way of wages and no more. But I think the *employé* has himself to blame for that. If you invoke the assistance of the law against your neighbour, that neighbour will give you precisely as much as the law compels him to give. Well, that is what organised Labour has done. It has its Trades Union, its Workmen's Compensation and Employers' Liability, and so on; and lately it has gouged out of a myopic Government a scheme of Old Age Pensions, to be eligible for which a man must on no account have exercised any kind of thrift throughout his working life. If he has, he is disqualified. All this legislation enables you to get the half-nelson on your employer. Under the circumstances you can hardly expect him to throw in benevolence as well. You can't have your cake and eat it. The old personal relations between master and man are dead—dead as Queen Anne—and with them has died the master's sense of moral responsibility for the welfare of those dependent on him."

"Time, too! Degradation! Feudal system!" observed the ever-ready Mr Killick.

"Well, perhaps; but the Feudal System had its points, Mr Killick. It fostered one or two homely and healthy virtues like benevolence and loyalty and pride of race; and I don't think a man-at-arms ever lost his self-respect or felt degraded because he lived in time of peace under the protection of the Lord of the Manor whom he followed in time of war. Yes, I for one rather regret the passing of the old order. Listen, and I will tell you a story. Forty years ago Cherry Hill Pit was flooded—flooded for nearly three months during a bitter hard winter. Sir Nigel Thompson's father, the late baronet—"

Sir Nigel, who was puzzling out some specially complicated formula, suddenly looked up. He had an idea that his name had been mentioned; but as every one present appeared to be listening most intently to the chairman, he resumed his engrossing occupation with a sigh of relief.

"—paid full wages during the whole of that time; and as coal was naturally unobtainable in the village, he imported sufficient to supply the needs of the whole community. Not a house in the village lacked its kitchen fire or its Sunday dinner during all those weeks. That was before the days of the Employers' Liability, gentlemen! If a similar disaster were to occur to-day, I doubt if Sir Nigel here would feel morally bound to do anything for such an independent and self-sufficient community. The present state of things may safeguard you against the ungenerous employer, but it eliminates the milk of human kindness from our mutual transactions, and that is always a matter for regret. That is all, gentlemen. You have our last word in this matter. These two men must go. If you would like to withdraw to the next room for a few minutes and consider whether you have anything further to say, we shall be glad to wait your convenience here."

The deputation rose and filed solemnly from the room, and the Board were left alone.

Presently Mr Aymer observed timidly—

"Mr Chairman, don't you think we might let Conlin stay, and content ourselves with dismissing Murton?"

"Afraid not," said Juggernaut. "It's a bit hard on Conlin, but we have to consider the greatest good of the greatest number. He's a plague-spot, and if we don't eradicate him he'll spread. Do you agree, Kirkley?"

"Bad luck on the poor devil, but I think you are right," assented his lordship.

"Crisp?"

Mr Crisp nodded.

"Nigel?"

Sir Nigel Thompson looked up from his seventh envelope with a contented sigh.

"I have it at last," he said. "It's a perfectly-simple solution, really, but the obvious often escapes one's notice owing to its very proximity. The eye is looking further afield. Eh—what? My decision? I agree implicitly with you, Jack—that is, gentlemen, I support the chairman in his view of the case."

And this vigilant counsellor collected his envelopes and stuffed them into his pocket. The chairman continued—

"Montague?"

"Before I answer that question," began Mr Montague, "I should like to protetht—protest, I mean—against the arbitrary manner in which you have conducted this meeting, Mr Chairman. You have taken the case out of our hands in a manner which I consider most unwarrantable; and, speaking as the actual employer of the two men—"

Juggernaut swung rather deliberately round in his chair.

"Mr Montague," he said, "you got yourself into a hole, and you called—no, _howled_—for a meeting of directors to come and pull you out. These agitators settled down in your district because they knew that it was the most fertile district to work in. You are considered, rightly, the worst employer of labour here. You are greedy, unscrupulous, and tyrannical. It is men like you who discredit Capital in the eyes of Labour, and make conciliatory dealing between master and man almost an impossibility. We have bolstered you up through a very difficult crisis, sitting here and putting those poor fellows, five of whom are infinitely more honest than you are, quite undeservedly in the wrong, and imperilling our immortal souls by whitewashing such employers as you. Accept the situation and be thankful!"

It is said that hard words break no bones. Still, if you happen to be a member of a race which has endured hard words (to say nothing of broken bones) for twenty centuries, and when the hard words on this particular occasion are delivered by a large man with angry blue eyes and a tongue like a whip-lash, you may be forgiven for losing your nerve a little. Mr Montague lost his. He flapped his ringed hands feebly, mumbled incoherently, and was understood to withdraw his objections unconditionally.

"Mr Amos Entwistle," announced a clerk at the door.

Entwistle junior re-entered the room.

"I am commissioned to inform you, Mr Chairman," he said, "that we acquiesce in your decision; but under protest. I should like to add, gentlemen," he continued, less formally but none the less earnestly, "that the Committee are very much dissatisfied with the result of the interview. I am afraid you haven't heard the last of this trouble. Good-day, and thank you, gentlemen!"

"What does it all mean? Strike—eh?" inquired Lord Kirkley, as he and Juggernaut descended the stairs together five minutes later.

"Perhaps. If so, we'll fight."

"Righto—I'm on! I say, it was pretty smart of you finding out where those private supplies of theirs came from last time. We shall be able to put the lid on that sort of think in future—what?"

Juggernaut nodded, but said no more.

Mr Crisp, Sir Nigel Thompson, and Mr Aymer walked across to the latter's offices for luncheon. Mr Montague had gone home to lunch by himself. He usually did so.

"The chairman arrived at the meeting in the nick of time," said the lawyer. "Kirkley would have been no match for Winch."

"The chairman was very inflexible," sighed Mr Aymer, with all a weak man's passion for compromise. "He has a way of brushing aside obstacles which can only be described as Napoleonic. Is he always within his rights from a legal point of view?"

"From a legal point of view, practically never," said the lawyer simply. "From a common-sense point of view, practically always."

"He is a hard man—as hard as flint," mused Mr Aymer. "I wonder if he has a soft side to him *anywhere*. I wonder, for instance, how he would treat a woman."

"I wonder," said Mr Crisp.

CHAPTER FOUR.

THE DEVIL A MONK WOULD BE.

The first member of the Rectory household whose eyes opened on Sunday morning was the Rector himself, who promptly arose and repaired to the church, there to conduct the early morning service. The second was a certain Mr Dawks, who has not previously been mentioned in this narrative. He was a dog. The term may include almost anything, which is perhaps fortunate for Mr Dawks; otherwise it might have been necessary to class him under some more elastic heading. Of his ancestry nothing was known, though many conjectures could have been made, and most of them would have been correct. He had been found lying half-dead in a country lane by Daphne six years ago, and though mistaken at the time for a derelict monkey jettisoned from some migratory hurdy-gurdy, had subsequently proved to be a mongrel puppy of a few months old. Regular meals and ripening years had developed him into a sort of general epitome of all the dogs that ever existed. He possessed points which, exhibited individually, would have gained many marks at Cruft's Dog-Show. His tail would have increased the market value of a Chow fourfold; his shoulders and forelegs would have done credit to a prize bull-terrier; his ears would have inflated the self-esteem of the silkiest spaniel in existence; and his lower jaw would have been regarded as an asset by an alligator. His manners were without reproach, but were derived rather from mental vacuity than nobility of character; for with the deportment of an hidalgo he combined the intelligence of a permanent official.

His name, as already mentioned, was Mr Dawks, but he responded with equal amiability to "Angel Child" or "Beautiful One" (Daphne); "Flea-Club" (Ally); "Puss, puss!" (Nicky); and "Tank-Engine" (Stiffy), to whose mechanical mind bandy legs and laboured breathing suggested a short wheel-base and leaky outside-cylinders.

Mr Dawks, having arisen from his nightly resting-place outside Daphne Vereker's bedroom door, strolled downstairs to the study. The Rector was frequently to be found there early in the morning, and were he not too deeply absorbed in some dusty volume, there might be biscuits. But the room was empty. Mr Dawks laboriously remounted the staircase and scratched delicately at his mistress's bedroom door.

He was admitted, and found Daphne, in dressing-gown and slippers, preparing for her Sunday morning round, in which she doubled the parts of what is known in the North of England as a "knocker-up" and mistress of the wardrobe; for the week's clean garments were always distributed on these occasions. The pair set forth together.

After a tap at her father's door, answered by a melodious "Good-morning, daughter!" which showed that the Rector had returned from his ministrations, Daphne proceeded to the regions above. Here upon the landing she encountered her youngest sister, who ought properly to have been dressing in the bedroom which she shared with Cilly. Instead, she was sitting resignedly outside the door upon a bundle composed of her Sabbath garments. As she was obviously posing for the excitation of sympathy, Daphne ignored her and passed into the bedroom, where the window-blind was flapping in the breeze and Cilly lay in a condition of almost total eclipse (if we except a long tawny pig-tail) under the bed-clothes.

"Cilly," inquired Daphne, "what's Nicky doing outside?"

"I kicked her out," replied a muffled voice.

"Why?"

"Well"—Cilly poked her head, tortoise-fashion, from under its covering—"she cheeked me—about"—the head retired again—"something."

"Bobby Gill, I suppose," remarked Daphne calmly.

Cilly's countenance reappeared, rosily flushed with healthy sleep and maiden modesty.

"Yes."

"Well, you must take her in again," said Daphne. "She's only playing up for a cold, sitting out there, and it will be a score for her if she can sniff the house down to-morrow."

"All right," said Cilly resignedly. "I suppose I can pay her out some other way."

"I wouldn't, if I were you," advised the elder sister. "She'll only wait till she gets you and Bobby together, and then say something *awful*. It's your own fault, dear. You do ask for it, you know."

Cilly, whose flirtations were more numerous than discreet, sighed deeply, and rolled a pair of large and dreamy eyes upon her sister.

"Daph, don't you *ever* fall in love with men? Well—boys, if you like!" she continued, parrying an unspoken comment. "I know I do overdo it a bit; but you—well, you never do it at all. Don't you love to feel them edging up to you, and getting pink in the face, and trying to think of things to say to you, and offering to take you—"

"No," said Daphne decidedly; "they bore me. Barring Dad and Mr Dawks and the boys, I have no use for males. Besides, I'm always too busy to bother with them: they waste so much of your time. Now, my child, if you want any breakfast you had better get up. I must go and see the boys."

She departed, and with a passing admonition to Nicky to abandon her eleemosynary vigil and be sure to wash her neck, continued on her way, still accompanied by the faithful Dawks, to the chamber occupied by her two youngest brothers.

Here peace reigned. Stiffy, one of whose chief joys in life was the study of the British Railway System, from Automatic Couplings to Newspaper Specials, was sitting up in bed with an old *Bradshaw*, laboriously ascertaining by how many routes and with how few changes the ordinary railway maniac might travel from Merthyr-Tydvil to Stockton-on-Tees. At the other end of the room the ever-occupied Anthony, with his night-shirt for a surplice and a stocking for a stole, was standing by an open grave (the hearthrug) rehearsing the opening passages of the Service for the Burial of the Dead,—an exercise to which, in common with various other ecclesiastical offices, he was much addicted.

Daphne, having kissed Stiffy and gravely given her verdict upon a knotty point which was exercising that scrupulous youth's mind, namely, whether it was permissible by the rules of the game to include in his schedule of connections a train which ran on Thursdays Only, handed him his weekly dole of clean linen and turned to the youngest member of the family.

"Good-morning, Tony dear," she said cheerfully.

The celebrant, who, true artist that he was, disliked unnecessary abruptness in his transitions, stopped short in the Ninetieth Psalm.

"Dearly Beloved Brethren," he gabbled in an apologetic undertone, "I am called for a moment from the side of this the last resting-place of our lamented sister"—apparently it was a lady friend he was interring—"by other business; but I shall be back in a minute." Then, unwinding the stocking from about his neck—

"Daphne, those new vests are beastly scratchy. Must I wear them?"

"I know, old man," responded his sister sympathetically. "But they've been bought and paid for—horribly dear, too!—so you must lump it. Try wearing them inside out for a time. That takes the edge off a bit."

And thus, with sage counsel and practical suggestion (together with a brief whistle to Mr Dawks, who was moistening his internal clay at the water-jug), our young Minerva passed on to the sleeping-place of her beloved Ally.

Rather to her surprise, Mr Aloysius Vereker was awake and out of bed. The reason was plain. Before him upon the dressing-table lay a pot of shaving-soap of a widely advertised brand, a new shaving-brush, a sixpenny bottle of bay rum, and a lather dish of red indiarubber,—youthful extravagances to which the hardened shaver of twenty years' standing, who smears himself with ordinary Brown Windsor out of the soap-dish and wipes his razor on a piece of newspaper or the window-curtain, looks back with mingled amusement and regret. In his hand gleamed a new razor.

"Careful!" he gasped through a sea of lather. "Don't shake the room, kid!"

Daphne sat cautiously down upon the bed, and surveyed the operator with unfeigned pride and enthusiasm. She clasped her hands.

"Ally, how splendid! When did you begin doing it?"

Ally, weathering a hairless and slippery corner, replied—

"Third time. I'm doing it chiefly to make something *grow*. A man simply *has* to shave after he gets into the Fifteen: you look such a fool on Saturday nights if you don't. A chap in our house called Mallock, who has had his colours four years, has a beard about half-an-inch long by Friday. He's a gorgeous sight."

Daphne shuddered slightly.

Ally continued.

"I don't expect to rival him, of course, but I should like to have something to scrape off in the dormitory. My fag always grins so when he brings me my shaving-water—little tick!"

Daphne was too well versed in the eccentricities of the young of the male species to experience the slightest feeling of surprise at her brother's singular ambition. She merely wrapped a blanket round her shoulders and settled herself against the head of the bed, anxiously contemplating the progress of a sanguinary campaign in the region surrounding Ally's jugular vein.

Presently operations came to a conclusion; the traces of battle were obliterated with much sponging and spraying; and the pair sat and gossiped amicably while Ally stropped his razor and put studs in his Sunday shirt.

It was a full quarter of an hour before Daphne returned to her room, for her Sunday morning call upon Ally was always a protracted affair. But before she left she had, after the usual blandishments, exacted from him a promise that he would come to church. Their father never exercised any compulsion in this matter; but if any member of the family did stay at home on Sunday morning, the Rector's mute distress was such as to blight the spirits of the household for the rest of the day; and Daphne always exerted herself to the full to round up her entire flock in the Rectory pew at the appointed hour. The most recalcitrant members thereof were Ally and Nicky, but the former could usually be cajoled and the latter coerced.

After breakfast the Rector retired to his study to con his sermon; and not long afterwards was to be seen, key in hand, passing through the wicket-gate which led from the garden into the churchyard. Having tolled the church bell for five minutes, he busied himself at the altar, and then turned up the lessons at the lectern, marking these same in plain figures; for the Squire, who fulfilled the office of reader, required careful guidance in this respect. (He had been known to read the same lesson twice; also the Second Lesson before the First; and once he had turned over two pages together towards the end of a long chapter, and embarked with growing huskiness and visible indignation upon a supplementary voyage of forty-seven verses.)

Presently the Rector returned to the house for his surplice; and ten minutes later, a tall and saintly figure, followed his hobnailed and bullet-headed choristers into the chancel.

Snayling Church, though a diminutive building, was one of the oldest of its kind in England. The tower was square and stumpy, and had served as a haven of refuge more than once. A later generation, following the pious but unnecessary fashion of the day, had erected upon its summit a steeple of homely design, which indicated the route to heaven in an officious and altogether gratuitous manner. Inside the building itself the roof was supported by massive stone pillars and Norman arches. Beneath the floor lay folk long dead, their names, virtues, and destination set forth in many curious inscriptions in stone and brass, all greatly prized by the tourist with his tracing-paper and heel-ball. The chancel contained a real Crusader, who reclined, sword in hand and feet crossed, upon a massive sarcophagus, his good lady by his side. Tony Vereker had woven many a legend about *him*, you may be sure.

Each of the tiny transepts contained two square pews, decently veiled from the public gaze by red curtains. Those on the north side belonged respectively to the Squire, whose arrival in church with his wife and four daughters always served as an intimation to the organist—Mr Pack, the schoolmaster—that it was eleven o'clock and time to wind up the voluntary; and old Lady Curlew of Hainings, who invariably arrived five minutes before the hour, accompanied by her maid; who, having packed her mistress into a corner of the pew with cushions and hassocks, retired discreetly to the free seats by the door.

Of the pews in the south transept one was the property of the Lord of the Manor, the Marquis of Kirkley. It was seldom occupied, for his lordship suffered from the misfortune (which modern legislation is doing so much to alleviate) of possessing more residences than he could comfortably live in. His adjacent seat, Kirkley Abbey, was seldom open except for a few weeks during the pheasant season; and even the recurrence of that momentous period did not postulate undue congestion in the family pew.

The other pew was the Rector's, and here Daphne succeeded on this particular Sabbath morning in corralling the full strength of her troupe.

Non sine pulvere, however. Ally, as already related, had proved fairly tractable, but Nicky (who just at present stood badly in need of the services of a competent exorcist) had almost evaded ecclesiastical conscription by a new and ingenious device. At ten-fifteen precisely she had fallen heavily down a flight of two steps and sprained her ankle. Unsympathetic Daphne, experienced in the detection of every form of malingering, had despatched her upstairs with a bottle of Mr Elliman's strongest embrocation—the property of Ally—with instructions to anoint the injured member and report herself for duty at ten-forty-five prompt. At the appointed hour Nicky, limping painfully and smiling heroically, had joined the rest of the family in the hall.

Presently Ally remarked casually—

"Rotten stink here. Furniture polish, or something."

"Yes—filthy reek!" agreed Stiffy.

"It's turpentine," cried Cilly, crinkling her nose.

"It's Elliman," said Tony.

"It's *you*, Nicky!" said everybody at once.

Daphne, who was drawing on her gloves, peeled them off again with some deliberation, and took her youngest sister by the shoulders.

"Nicky," she inquired, "how much Elliman did you use?"

That infant martyr, wincing ostentatiously, delicately protruded a foot, and exhibited a long black leg heavily swathed from knee to instep under her stocking with a bandage of colossal dimensions.

"Not more than I could help, Daph," she said. "I found one or two other bruises on my—all over me, in fact: so I—I just put a little Elliman on each. I didn't want to be a trouble to any one, so—"

"Run upstairs, Stiffy," Daphne interpolated swiftly, "and see how much Elliman is left in the bottle."

By this time Cilly had thrown open the front door and staircase windows, and the remainder of the Vereker family were fanning themselves with their Sunday hats and ostentatiously fighting for breath—an exercise in which they persevered until Stiffy reappeared carrying an empty bottle.

"Two bobs' worth!" shouted Ally. "And I meant it to last for months! Nicky, you little *sweep!*"

Daphne glanced at the hall clock.

"Fourteen minutes!" she calculated frantically. "Yes, it can just be done. Nicky, my cherub, you shall come to church this morning if I have to *scrape* you. Go on, you others! I'll follow myself as quickly as I can."

The last sentence was delivered far up the staircase, which Miss Vereker was ascending with flying feet, a tearful and unwilling appendage trailing behind her. Next moment the bathroom door banged, and the departing worshippers heard both taps turned on.

———

At two minutes past eleven precisely Daphne and Nicky, the former cool, collected, and as prettily dressed as any woman in the congregation, the latter scarlet as if from recent parboiling, walked demurely down the aisle just as the choir entered the chancel, lustily bellowing a hymn which drew attention to the advantages accruing in the next world to that Servant of the Lord who should be found Waiting in his Office, in a Posture not specified—Tony used often to wonder what would happen if the Day of Judgment should fall upon a Bank holiday or Saturday afternoon—and joined the rest of the family in the Rectory pew.

———

A sermon, we all know, offers unique facilities for quiet reflection. As their father's silvery voice rose and fell in the cadences of his discourse—he had soared far above the heads of his bucolic audience, and was now disporting himself in a delectable but quite inaccessible æther of his own, where the worshippers (such of them as had not yielded to slothful repose) followed his evolutions with mystified and respectful awe, much as a crowd of citizens in a busy street gape upwards at the gambols of an aeroplane—the Rectory children wedged themselves into their own particular nooks of the pew, and prepared to get through the next twenty minutes in characteristic fashion.

Ally closed his eyes and assumed an attitude of slumber, as befitted his years and dignity. But he was not asleep. He did not look comfortable. Perhaps his breakfast had disagreed with him, or possibly he was contemplating within himself the vision of a receding University and an all-too-adjacent office-stool. Daphne, with her eyes fixed on the wall opposite and her brow puckered, was pondering some domestic problem—her own extravagantly small feet, mayhap, or Wednesday's hypothetical leg of mutton. Despite her burden of care, her face looked absurdly round and childish under her big beaver hat. One hand supported her chin in a characteristic pose, the other controlled the movements of the restless Anthony, who was impersonating something of a vibratory nature. Cilly, with glowing eyes and parted lips, was reading the Marriage Service in her Prayerbook. Nicky, whose recent ablutions had apparently purged her of outward sin only, had pulled forward two long wisps of black hair from behind her ears, and by crossing these under her nose had provided herself with a very realistic and terrifying pair of moustaches, by portentous twistings of which, assisted by the rolling of a frenzied eye, she was endeavouring to make poor Stiffy laugh. That right-minded youth, though hard pressed, had so far withstood temptation by resolutely reciting to himself a favourite excerpt from Bradshaw's Railway Guide, beginning "Brighton (Central), Preston Park, Burgess Hill, Hassocks" ... and ending with ... "Grosvenor Road, Victoria,"—a sedative exercise to which he was much addicted at moments of bodily anguish or mental stress; but it was plain that his defence was weakening.

Fortunately, the approaching explosion, which would have been of a cataclysmal nature,—Stiffy was not a boy to do things by halves,—was averted by a change of demeanour on the part of the temptress. Her quick ear had caught some unaccustomed sound behind her. Letting go her moustaches, which immediately assumed a more usual position, she squirmed round in her seat and gently parted the red rep curtains which separated the Rectory pew from that of Kirkley Abbey. An excited gurgle apprised her fellow-worshippers of the fact that some unusual sight had met her eyes.

What Nicky saw was this.

Immediately opposite to her improvised peep-hole sat a man—a large man with square shoulders and an immobile face. He was clean-shaven, with two strong lines running from his nostrils to the corners of his mouth—a mouth which even in repose looked determined and grim. He possessed a square jaw and rather craggy brows. It was difficult to decide if he were sleeping or no, for though his eyes were closed there was none of the abandon of slumber about his pose. His most noticeable feature was the set of his eyebrows, which, instead of being arched or level, ran upwards and outwards in a diagonal direction, and gave him a distinctly Satanic appearance—a circumstance which Nicky noted with sympathetic approval. He was dressed in the somewhat *dégagé* Sabbath attire affected by

Englishmen spending the week-end in the country, and his feet were perched upon the seat opposite to him.

Presently, for some cause unknown—possibly Nicky's hard breathing—he opened his eyes.

Immediately in front of him the stranger beheld a small excited face, a pair of saucer-like blue eyes, and a wide but attractive mouth—the whole vision framed in dusty red rep. The face was flushed, the eyes glowed, and the mouth was wide open.

The picture, suddenly surprised in its inspection by a pair of the shrewdest and most penetrating eyes it had ever beheld, dropped hurriedly out of its frame and disappeared. If Nicky had waited a moment longer she would have received a less one-sided impression of the stranger, for almost simultaneously with the discovery of the apparition in the peep-hole the man smiled. Instantly his whole face changed. The outer corners of his eyebrows descended, the crease between them disappeared, and magnificent teeth gleamed for a moment in the dim religious light of the pew.

Nicky leaned across to her eldest sister and whispered huskily:—

"There's somebody in the other pew. I think it's the Devil. Look yourself!"

But Daphne, deep in domestic mental arithmetic, smiled and shook her head; and Nicky received little more encouragement from the rest of the family. The profession of scare-monger and exploiter of mares' nests, though enjoyable on the whole, has its drawbacks: if you get hold of a genuine scare or an authentic mare's nest, nobody believes you.

The sermon began to draw to a close, and a few minutes later the Rector descended from the clouds and gave out the final hymn, prefacing his announcement by an intimation that the offertory that day would be devoted to the needs of the Children's Cottage Hospital in the neighbouring county town. His appeal was characteristic.

"Money," he mused, "is the most hampering and perplexing thing in this life. It is so artificial and unnecessary. I often sigh for a world where all commerce will be in kind—where a cheque on the Bank of Gratitude will settle the weekly bills, and 'I thank you!' be regarded as legal tender up to any amount. But there is no give and take in these days. Everything, from Life and Love down to the raiment we wear, is duly appraised and ticketed, and if we stand in need of these things we must render a material tale of pounds and pence or go without. No wonder men call this the Iron Age! But, though money as a rule brings nothing in its train but disappointment and regret (and therefore it is better to have too little than too much), there are times and seasons when it is permitted to us to purchase happiness with it. To-day gives us one of these opportunities. Do not let that opportunity slip. *Post est Occasio calva.*" (Respectful intake of breath on the part of the congregation.) "I do not urge you to give on the plea put forward in a hymn that you will find in your books—a hymn written by a man who should have known better—a hymn which shall never, so long as I am Rector of this parish, emerge from the obscurity of the printed page—advocating generosity in almsgiving on the ground that contributions to the offertory on earth will be refunded at the rate of a hundred thousand per cent in heaven. I do not ask you to give either much or little. Very few of us here are over-burdened with this world's goods. Still, we can each afford to buy *some* happiness to-day, at a very low rate. And it will not be transitory or temporary happiness either; for every time hereafter that your daily task or a country walk takes you past the Children's Hospital at Tilney, that happiness will blossom again with ever-reviving fragrance in your hearts. Let us sing Hymn number three hundred and sixty-nine—

'Thine arm, O Lord, in days of old
Was strong to heal and save....'"

There was a general upheaval of the congregation and a clatter of rustic boots; the little organ gave a premonitory rumble, and the hymn began.

The hymn after the sermon is not, as a rule—to-day was an exception—an impressive canticle. *Imprimis*, it is of abnormal length and little coherence, having apparently been composed for the sole purpose of lasting out the collection of the offertory; *item*, the congregation is furtively engaged in retrieving umbrellas from under seats and gliding into overcoats. Hence it was always a pleasant diversion to the Rectory children to follow the movements of the two churchwardens as they ran their godly race up the aisle in the pursuit of alms and oblations. They even risked small sums on the result. When the Squire and Mr Murgatroyd (Stationer and Dealer in Fancy Goods) stepped majestically from their respective pews and set to work on this particular morning, Daphne produced five sixpences and handed them to her brothers and sisters. Nicky, in her anxiety to see what sum the stranger in the Kirkley Abbey pew would contribute to the total, received her own contribution with such nonchalance that the coin slipped from her hand, and was being hunted for among hassocks upon the floor at the moment when Mr Murgatroyd reached the stranger's pew.

Nicky found her sixpence, and resumed an upright attitude just in time to hear (in a pause between two verses) a faint papery rustle on the other side of the curtain.

A moment later Mr Murgatroyd opened the door of the Rectory pew, with his usual friendly air of dropping in for a cup of tea, and presented the bag.

The children put in their sixpences one by one. Nicky's turn came last. She peered into the bag, and her sharp eyes caught sight of something white protruding from amid the silver and copper.

Taking the bag from Mr Murgatroyd's hands—she controlled that indulgent bachelor as she willed: he counted it a pleasure to turn his stock inside out on a Saturday afternoon whenever Miss Veronica came in with a penny to spend—Nicky deliberately drew out a piece of folded crinkly white paper. This, laying the offertory bag upon the baize-covered table in the middle of the pew, she carefully unfolded, and perused the staring black legend inscribed upon the flimsy white background. When she raised her eyes they were those of an owlet suffering from mental shock.

"Golly!" she observed in bell-like tones. "The Devil has put in a ten-pound note!"

CHAPTER FIVE.

A SABBATH-DAY'S JOURNEY.

The Rectory children, washed and combed for Sunday dinner, sat at ease in the old nursery—promoted to schoolroom since Tony went into knickerbockers—and discussed the munificent stranger of the morning.

Their interest in his movements and identity had been heightened by the fact that after service was over he had proceeded to the right instead of the left on leaving the Kirkley Abbey pew, and, turning his broad back upon an undisguisedly interested congregation, had stalked up the chancel and disappeared through the door leading to the vestry.

"I *wonder* what he went for," said Cilly for the third time.

"Perhaps he was going to give Dad more banknotes," suggested the optimistic Stiffy.

"More likely going to ask for change out of the first one," rejoined Ally, the cynic.

"I expect he was going to complain about you making faces at him through the curtain, Nicky," coldly observed Cilly, who had not yet forgiven her small sister's innuendoes on the subject of Mr Robert Gill.

"Rats!" demurred Nicky uneasily. "I didn't make faces. I expect he's only some tourist who wants to rub brasses, or sniff a vault, or something."

"He must be a friend of Lord Kirkley's," said Ally, "because—"

"*I'll* show you who he is," shrilled a voice from the depth of a cupboard under the window.

Tony, who had been grubbing among a heap of tattered and dusty literature in the bottom shelf, now rose to his feet and staggered across the room carrying an ancient but valuable copy of 'The Pilgrim's Progress,' embellished with steel engravings.

Having deposited the volume upon the hearthrug he proceeded to hunt through its pages. Presently, with a squeal of delight, he placed a stumpy fore-finger upon a full-page illustration, and announced triumphantly—

"That's him!"

The picture represented Christian's battle with Apollyon. Christian, hard pressed, had been beaten to his knees, and over him towered the figure of the Prince of Darkness, brandishing a sword and (in the most unsportsmanlike manner) emitting metallic-looking flames from his stomach. The children gathered round.

"You are right, Tony," said Cilly at length, "it *is* like him."

Certainly Apollyon bore a sort of far-away resemblance to the late occupant of the Kirkley Abbey pew.

"Look at his eyebrows," said Nicky, "they go straight up—"

The churchyard gate clicked, and voices were heard in conversation outside. Daphne sped to the window.

"Heavens!" she exclaimed in an agonised whisper, "Dad is bringing him in to lunch! Ally, take your boots off the mantelpiece! Nicky, pull up your stockings! Cilly, knock Dawks off the sofa! I must fly. I wonder if there's enough cream to make a trifle. Anyhow, the beef—"

And she sped away kitchenwards like an agitated butterfly.

A few minutes later the Rector appeared in the schoolroom, smiling joyously, with his hand resting lightly on the shoulder of the recently identified Apollyon. Tony was restoring 'The Pilgrim's Progress' to its shelf with the complacency of a second Bertillon.

"These are my flock, Jack," said Brian Vereker. "I wonder if any of you children can guess who this gentleman is? Would you think that he and I were at school together? Tony, I have often told you of little Jack Carr, who used to light my fire and cook my breakfast. And a shocking mess he used to make of it, eh? Didn't you, Jack? Do you remember the day you fried sausages in marmalade, because the label on the pot said marmalade would be found an excellent substitute for butter? Well, here he is, Tony. We have run together again after twenty-five years. Come and shake hands. These are my two younger girls, Jack, and these are my three boys. Where is Daphne, children?"

The Vereker family, drawn up in a self-conscious row, were understood to intimate that Daphne was downstairs. A move was therefore made in the direction of the dining-room, where Keziah, the little maid, was heatedly laying an extra place. Daphne joined the party a moment later, and welcomed Sir John Carr—such was his full title, it appeared—with prettiness and composure. But Cilly and Nicky noted that she had found time to rearrange her hair in honour of the occasion, and adorn herself with most of her slender stock of jewellery—two bangles and a thin gold chain.

Sunday dinner was something of a function at the Rectory. For one thing there was hot roast beef, which counts for much when you see the like only once in the week. The Rector carved and Stiffy handed round the plates, Keziah, whose Sunday-afternoon-out commenced technically the moment the sirloin was dished, being excused from further attendance. Daphne presided over the vegetable dishes and Ally cut bread at the sideboard. The office of butler was in abeyance, for the Vereker family drank only water from their highly polished christening-mugs. Nicky was responsible for the table-napkins, and Cilly mixed salads in season.

All these domestic details Daphne explained, with captivating friendliness and a freedom from self-consciousness that many a more matured hostess might have envied, to the silent man beside her.

"Sorry to have *all* the family pouring things over you," she said, as Stiffy with a plate of beef, Ally with a lump of bread impaled upon a fork, and Cilly with a bowl of lettuce, egg, and beetroot cunningly intermingled, converged simultaneously upon the guest; "but we have only one servant, and——"

Stephen Blasius Vereker, poised upon his toes and holding his breath, was leaning heavily over the guest's right shoulder, proffering a platter upon the edge of which a billow of gravy, piling itself up into a tidal wave, strove to overcome the restraining influence of surface tension. Apollyon, his features unrelaxed, gravely took the plate, and restoring it to a horizontal position, turned deferentially to resume his conversation with his young hostess.

——"And I like poor Keziah to have as long a Sunday out as possible," continued Daphne, entirely unruffled.

"Her young man waits for her at the stile down by Preston's farm," supplemented Nicky. "They go for a walk down Tinkler's Den, and never speak a *word* to each other."

——"So we wait on ourselves at this meal," concluded Daphne. "What will you drink, Sir John? Father is a teetotaller, and so are all of us; but if you are not, I've got some brandy upstairs in the nursery medicine cupboard."

"Thank you, I will drink water," said Sir John solemnly.

By this time the Vereker family had settled down to their own portions, and were babbling as cheerfully and unrestrainedly as usual. Shyness in the presence of strangers was not one of their weaknesses, and presently, taking advantage of Daphne's departure to the kitchen in quest of the second course, they engaged their guest in conversation, inviting his opinions on such widely different subjects as the quality of the salad (Cilly), the merits of the automatic vacuum railway brake as compared with those of the Westinghouse (Stiffy), and the prospects of Cambridge in the coming Boat

Race (Ally). All of which queries were answered in a fashion which, while lacking in geniality and erring a little on the side of terseness, showed that the respondent knew what he was talking about.

The Rector, at the head of the table, smiled benignantly. To him this reticent man of over forty, with the deep-set eyes and square jaw, was the sturdy chubby boy who had cooked his breakfast and worshipped him from afar in the dim but joyous days when Brian Vereker was a giant of nineteen, with side whiskers, and Jacky Carr a humble fag of twelve. It was almost a shock to hear him offered spirits to drink.

Presently Daphne returned, and another general post ensued, at the end of which the beef and vegetables had disappeared, and a suet pudding (the standing Sabbath sweet at the Rectory), flanked by a dish of trifle of diminutive proportions, lay before the hostess. The Rector was confronted by a melon.

Taking advantage of a covering conversation between the guest and her eldest brother, Miss Vereker made a mysterious pass over the surface of the trifle with a spoon, while she murmured to such of the family as were within earshot the mystic formula, "F. H. B.!" Then she inquired aloud—

"Cilly, dear, which pudding will you have?"

"Baby Maud, please," replied Miss Cecilia promptly, indicating the stiff, pallid, and corpse-like cylinder of suet.

She was helped, and Nicky's choice was ascertained.

"I don't *think*," that damsel replied sedately, "that I'll have anything, thank you, Daphne. I'm not very hungry to-day."

Daphne, with a slight twitch at the corners of her mouth—she appreciated Nicky's crooked little ways, despite herself—turned to the guest.

"Will you have pudding or trifle, Sir John? Let me recommend the trifle."

"Thank you, I never eat sweets," was the reply.

An audible sigh of relief rose from the Messrs Vereker.

"Daph, dear," said Nicky before any one else could speak, "I think I'll change my mind and have some trifle."

And thus, by prompt generalship, Miss Veronica Vereker, while obeying to the letter the laws of hospitality and precedence, stole a march upon her slow-moving brethren and sisters and received the lion's share of the trifle, the balance going to Tony by virtue of juniority.

As Daphne handed her triumphant little sister her portion, she distinctly heard a muffled sound on her right.

"I like this man!" she said to herself.

"If you don't take sweets, Jack," observed the Rector from the other end of the table, "allow me to introduce you to this melon—a present from the Squire. Take the melon round to Sir John, Stiffy, and he shall cut in where he pleases; though, strictly speaking," he added, with simple enjoyment of his own joke, "it is hardly etiquette to cut anything you have been introduced to!"

There was a momentary stoppage in the general mastication of "Baby Maud," and the right hand of each Vereker present performed the same evolution. Next moment the repast was resumed, but the guest observed, not without surprise, that every christening-mug—even Daphne's—had a knife lying across its top.

"That is one of our customs," explained Cilly politely. "We do it whenever any one makes a stale joke."

"*Alice through the Looking-Glass*," corroborated Nicky, scooping up trifle with an air of severe reproof—"page two hundred and seven."

"You see my servile and dependent position in this house, Jack!" said the Rector, not altogether dejectedly.

"I perceive that I have dropped into a Republic," said Sir John Carr.

"Republic? A more absolute despotism never existed. Wait until you have transgressed one of the Laws of the Medes and Persians and been brought up for judgment before my eldest daughter? *We* know, don't we—eh, Nicky?"

Brian Vereker projected the furtive smile of a fellow-conspirator upon his youngest daughter, and then turned to gaze with unconcealed fondness and pride upon his eldest.

"I trust that when I transgress," said Sir John, "I shall get off under the First Offender's Act."

"You have broken that already," said Daphne readily; "but it's Dad's fault. It is twenty minutes to three, and you two ought to have been smoking in the study ten minutes ago instead of talking here. I want to get this room cleared for the children to learn their Catechism in."

At half-past three Brian Vereker summoned his eldest daughter to the study, and announced with frank delight that Sir John Carr had agreed to vacate the Kirkley Arms and accept the hospitality of the Rectory.

"I am going to walk down to the inn now," said Apollyon to Daphne, "to see about my luggage. Perhaps you will keep me company?"

"All right," said Daphne. "I'll bring Mr Dawks too. He wants a walk, I know."

Sir John made no comment, but gave no active support to the inclusion of Mr Dawks in the party. It may be noted, however, that when Daphne had at length achieved that feat which encroaches so heavily upon a woman's share of eternity—the putting on of her hat—and joined her guest in the garden accompanied by Mr Dawks in person, Apollyon greeted the owner of the name with far more cordiality than he had greeted the name itself. It is sometimes misleading to bestow Christian titles upon dumb animals.

Once away from the rest of the family, Daphne's maternal solemnity fell from her like a schoolmaster's cap and gown in holiday time. She chattered like a magpie, pointing out such objects of local interest as—
    (1) Farmer Preston's prize bull;
    (2) The residence of a reputed witch;
    (3) A spinney, where a dog-fox had once gone to ground at one end of an earth and a laughing hyena (subsequently ascertained to be the lost property of that peripatetic nobleman Lord George Sanger) had emerged from the other, to the entire and instantaneous disintegration of a non-abstaining local Hunt.

"I say, where do you live?" she inquired suddenly, breaking off in the middle of a detailed history of Kirkley Abbey, whose *façade* could be discerned through the trees on their right—"London?"

"Yes."

"All the year round?"

"No. I spend a good deal of my time in the North."

"Oh. What do you do there? What *are* you, by the way?" Daphne looked up at her companion with bird-like inquisitiveness. She moved in a society familiar with the age, ancestry, profession, wardrobe, ailments, love affairs, and income of every one within a radius of five miles. Consequently she considered a new acquaintanceship incomplete in the last degree until she had acquired sufficient information on the subject in hand to supply, say, a tolerably intimate obituary notice.

"I suppose you are *something*," she continued. "I hope so, anyhow. An idle man is always so mopy."

"What would you put me down as?" asked Apollyon.

Daphne scrutinised him without fear or embarrassment.

"I'm not much of a judge," she said. "You see, we don't come across many men here, and we are so poor that we don't get away much."

"Don't you go up to London occasionally, to buy a new frock?" said Sir John, covertly regarding the trim figure by his side.

"Me—London? Not much. Dad has a lot of grand relations there, but I don't think he bothered much about them, or they about him, after he married. He was too much wrapped up in mother. So we never hear anything of them now. No, I have hardly ever been away from Snayling, and I'm a great deal too busy here to worry about London or any other such place. So I don't know much about men," she concluded simply— "except my own, of course."

"Your own?"

"Yes—Dad and the boys. And then I know all about the sort of man one meets round here. I can tell a ditcher from a ploughman; and if I meet a man in a dog-cart with cases at the back I know he's a commercial traveller, and if he has a red face I know he's a farmer, and if he hasn't I know he's a doctor; but I haven't had much other experience."

"Still, what am *I*?" reiterated Apollyon.

"Well—I suppose you are not a soldier, or you would have a moustache."

"No."

"You might be a lawyer, being clean-shaven. Are you?"

"No."

"Oh! That's rather disappointing. You would make a ripping judge, with a big wig on. Well, perhaps you write things. I know—you are an author or an editor?"

"No."

"Foiled again!" said Daphne cheerfully. "Let me see, what other professions are there? Are you a Don, by any chance? A fellow, or lecturer, or anything? We had a Fellow of All Souls down here once. He was a dear."

"No."

"You are a 'Varsity man, I suppose."

"Yes."

"Oxford or Cambridge?"

"Cambridge."

"I am glad. Dark blue is *so* dull, isn't it? Besides, Dad is a Cambridge man. He is an old Running Blue. He won—but of course you know all about that. It seems queer to think you knew him before I did! Well, I give you up. What *do* you do?"

Apollyon reflected.

"I sell coals," he replied at last, rather unexpectedly.

This announcement, and the manner in which it was made, momentarily deprived Miss Vereker of speech—a somewhat rare occurrence.

"I see," she said presently. "We get ours from the station-master," she added politely.

"I was not proposing to apply for your custom," said Apollyon meekly.

At this point they reached the Kirkley Arms, and in the effort involved in rousing that somnolent hostelry from its Sabbath coma and making arrangements for the sending up of Sir John Carr's luggage to the Rectory, the question of why he sold coals, and whether he hawked the same round in a barrow or delivered his wares through the medium of the Parcels Post, was lost sight of.

On the homeward walk conversation was maintained on much the same terms. Daphne held forth unwearyingly, and Apollyon contented himself for the most part with answering her point-blank questions and putting a few—a very few—of his own. Certainly the man was a born listener, and amazingly magnetic. Tacitus himself could not have said less, and the greatest cross-examiner in the legal profession could not have extracted more. As they strolled side by side through the Kirkley woods, where the last of the daffodils were reluctantly making way for the first of the primroses, Daphne found herself reciting, as to a discreet and dependable father-confessor, a confidential but whole-hearted summary of the present state of domestic politics.

Ally's failure to secure a scholarship at the University was mentioned.

It was disgusting of him to miss the Greek Prose paper, Daphne considered. "He didn't oversleep at all, of course. I soon found *that* out. The real reason was that he had gone to some man's rooms the night before, and the silly brat must go and drink a whisky-and-soda and smoke a cigar. That did it! It was no use telling Dad, because he simply wouldn't believe such a story; and if he did, it would make him unhappy for weeks. Besides, who can blame the poor dear? You can't be surprised if a schoolboy kicks over the traces a bit the first time he finds himself out on his own—can you?"

"I thought," replied Sir John, finding that some answer was expected of him, "that you said you knew nothing of men?"

"I said I didn't know *many* men," corrected Daphne. "But those I do know I know pretty thoroughly. They're very easy to understand, dear things! You always know where you are with them. Now, girls are different. Did you notice that boy whom we passed just now, who went pink and took off his hat. That's Bobby Gill—a flame of Cilly's. I'm going to have a lot of trouble with Cilly's love-affairs, I can see. She falls down and worships every second man she meets. I believe she would start mooning round the place after *you* if you weren't so old," she added. "Cilly's a darling, but what she wants——"

She plunged, with puckered brow and tireless tongue, into a further tale of hopes and fears. Stiffy's schooling, Nicky's boots, the curate who *had* to come—all were laid upon the table. Even the Emergency Bag and Wednesday's joint crept in somehow.

They were almost home when she concluded.

Suddenly Apollyon inquired:

"Do you know the name of that little hollow on our right? Is it Tinkler's Den?"

"Yes; we often have picnics there. How did you know?"

"It is part of Lord Kirkley's estate, as you are probably aware; and his lordship, finding like most of us that he has not sufficient money for his needs, has asked me to come and have a look at the ground round Tinkler's Den on the off-chance of our finding coal there."

Daphne turned upon him, wide-eyed and horror-struck.

"You mean to say," she gasped, "that you are going to dig for coals in Tinkler's Den?"

"I can't tell you, until——"

Apollyon paused. A small hand was resting on his sleeve, and a very small voice said beseechingly—

"Don't—*please!*"

"Very well, then: I won't," he said, in a matter-of-fact fashion; and they resumed their walk.

"I hope you haven't been bored," said Daphne, the hostess in her rising to the surface as the shadow of the Rectory fell upon her once more. "Your ears must be simply aching, but it's such a treat to talk to any one who knows about things. I never get the chance to ask advice. I usually have to give it. Dad and the boys are so helpless, bless them!"

They were passing through the wicket-gate. Daphne suddenly paused, and looked up at her guest with more mischief in her eyes than her brothers and sisters would have given her credit for.

"It's queer," she mused, "that you should sell coals. *We* thought you *shovelled* them!"

"Explain, please!" said Sir John.

Daphne did so. "We *had* to call you something," she concluded apologetically. "Do you mind?"

"Not at all. I have been called a good many names in my time," said Sir John grimly.

"What do your friends call you?" asked Daphne—"your intimate friends."

"I am not sure that I have any."

Daphne surveyed him shrewdly, with her head a little on one side.

"No—I should think you *were* that sort," she said gravely. "Well, what do your—do other people call you?"

"Most of them, I believe," said Sir John, "call me 'Juggernaut Carr.'"

CHAPTER SIX.

DAPHNE AS MATCHMAKER.

Juggernaut's stay at the Rectory had been prolonged for more than three weeks, the business upon which he was engaged being as easily directed, so he said, from Brian Vereker's study as from his own London offices. An unprejudiced observer might have been forgiven for remarking that to all appearances it could have been directed with equal facility from the Two-penny Tube or the North Pole; for if we except a prolonged interview with Lord Kirkley's land agent on the second day after his arrival, Juggernaut's activities had been limited to meditative contemplation of the Rector's spring flowers and some rather silent country walks in company with the lady to whom the Rector was wont to refer to in his playful moments as "my elderly ugly daughter."

Whether Daphne's impulsive protest against the desecration of her beloved Tinkler's Den carried weight, or whether that sylvan spot was found wanting in combustible properties, will never be known; but it may be noted here that Lord Kirkley was advised that there was no money in his scheme, and Snayling remains an agricultural centre to this day.

However, if it be a fact that no fresh experience can be altogether valueless, Juggernaut's time was certainly not wasted. He was absorbed into the primitive civilisation of Snayling Rectory. He was initiated into tribal custom and usage, and became versed in a tribal language consisting chiefly of abbreviations and portmanteau words. He was instructed in the principles which underlie such things as precedence in the use of the bath and helpings at dinner. He also studied with interest the fundamental laws governing the inheritance of out-grown garments. Having been born without brothers and sisters, he found himself confronted for the first time with some of those stern realities and unavoidable hardships which prevail when domestic supply falls short of domestic demand. The mystic phrase "F. H. B.!" for instance, with which Daphne had laid inviolable taboo upon the trifle on the day of his arrival, he soon learned stood for "Family, hold back!"

Again, if Master Stephen Blasius Vereker suggested to Miss Veronica Elizabeth Vereker that a B. O. at the T. S. would be an L. B. of A. R.; to which the lady replied gently but insistently, "Is it E. P.?" Juggernaut was soon able to understand that in response to an intimation on the part of her brother that a Blow Out at the Tuck Shop would be a Little Bit of All

Right, the cautious and mercenary damsel was inquiring whether her Expenses would be Paid at the forthcoming orgy. If Stiffy continued, "Up to 2 D.," and Nicky replied, "If you can't make it a tanner, Stiffy, darling, je pense *ne!*" the visitor gathered without much difficulty that in the opinion of Miss Veronica no gentleman worthy of the name should presume to undertake the entertainment of a lady under a minimum outlay of sixpence.

Juggernaut soon settled down to the ways of the establishment. He said little, but it was obvious, even to the boys, that he was taking a good deal in. He seldom asked questions, but he possessed an uncanny knack of interpreting for himself the most secret signs and cryptic expressions of the community. This established for him a claim to the family's respect, and in acknowledgment of the good impression he had created he was informally raised from the status of honoured guest to that of familiar friend. What the Associated Body of Colliery Owners would have thought if they could have seen their chairman meekly taking his seat at the breakfast-table, what time the family, accompanying themselves with teaspoons against teacups, chanted a brief but pointed ditty consisting entirely of the phrase "pom-pom!" repeated *con amore* and *sforzando* until breathlessness intervened—an ordeal known at the Rectory as "pom-pomming," and inflicted daily upon the last to appear at breakfast—is hard to say. Mr Montague for one would have enjoyed it.

Only once did this silent and saturnine man exhibit any flash of feeling. One morning before breakfast Daphne, busy in the knife-and-boot shed at the back of the house, heard a step on the gravel outside, and Juggernaut stood before her.

"Good-morning!" she said cheerfully. "Excuse my get-up. I expect I look rather a ticket."

Juggernaut surveyed her. She wore a large green baize apron. Her skirt was short and business-like, and her sleeves were rolled up above the elbow. Her hair was twisted into a knot at the back of her head. Plainly her toilet had only reached the stage of the *petit lever*. She was engaged in the healthful but unfashionable occupation of blacking boots; *per contra*, what Juggernaut chiefly noted was the whiteness of her arms. Finally his eye wandered to the boot in which her left hand was engulfed.

"Whose boot is that?" he asked.

"Yours, I should say. Dad's are square in the toes."

Next moment a large and sinewy hand gripped her by the wrist, and the boot was taken from her.

"Understand," said Apollyon, looking very like Apollyon indeed, "this must never occur again. I am angry with you."

He spoke quite quietly, but there was a vibrant note in his voice which Daphne had never heard before. Mr Tom Winch and Mr Montague would have recognised it. She looked up at him fearlessly, rather interested than otherwise in this new side of his character.

"I can't quite grasp why you *should* be angry," she said, "though I can see you are. Not being millionaires, we all clean our own boots—excepting Dad, of course. I always do his. You being a visitor, I threw yours in as a make-weight. It's all in the day's work."

But Juggernaut's fit had passed.

"I beg your pardon," he said. "I have no right to be angry with any one but myself. I am ashamed. I should have thought about this sooner, but I accepted your assurance that my visit would throw no extra burden upon the household rather too readily. Now, for the rest of the time I am here I propose, with your permission, to black my own boots. And as a sort of compensation for the trouble I have caused, I am going to black my hostess's as well."

"Do you know *how* to?" inquired the hostess, rather apprehensively.

For answer Juggernaut picked up a laced shoe from off the bench and set to work upon it.

"I once blacked my own boots every day for two years," he said, breathing heavily upon the shoe. "Now, if you want to go in and superintend the preparation of breakfast, you may leave me here, and I will undertake to produce the requisite standard of brilliancy." His face lit up with one of his rare and illuminating smiles, and he set grimly to work again.

Daphne hesitated for a moment, and surveyed her guest doubtfully. He was burnishing her shoe in a manner only to be expected of an intensely active man who has been utterly idle for a fortnight. His face was set in the lines which usually appeared when he was driving business through a refractory meeting. Daphne turned and left the boot-house, unpinning her apron and whistling softly.

Juggernaut finished off her shoes with meticulous care, and putting them back upon the bench turned his attention to his own boots. But his energy was plainly flagging. Several times his hand was stayed, and his eye wandered in the direction of his hostess's shoes. They were a remarkably neat pair. Daphne was proud of her feet—they were her only real vanity—and she spent more upon her boots and shoes than the extremely limited sum voted for the purpose by her conscience. More than once Juggernaut laid aside his own property and returned to the highly unnecessary task of painting the lily—if such a phrase can be applied to the efficient blacking of a shoe. Finally he picked up his boots and departed, to endure a pom-pomming of the most whole-hearted description on his appearance at the breakfast table.

But henceforth he found his way to the boot-house every morning at seven-thirty, where, despite his hostess's protests, he grimly carried out his expressed intention.

This was the only occasion, however, on which he asserted his will with Daphne. In all else she found him perfectly amenable. He permitted her without protest to overhaul his wardrobe, and submitted meekly to a scathing lecture upon the negligence apparent in the perforated condition of some of his garments and the extravagance evinced by the multiplicity of others. In short, Daphne adopted Juggernaut, as only a young and heart-whole girl can whose experience of men so far has been purely domestic. She felt like his mother. To her he was a child of the largest possible growth, who, not having enjoyed such advantages as she had all her life bestowed upon the rest of the flock, must needs be treated with twofold energy and special consideration. He was her Benjamin, she felt.

Juggernaut was to depart to-morrow. His socks were darned. Items of his wardrobe, hitherto anonymous, were neatly marked with his initials. His very pocket-handkerchiefs were numbered.

"You are sending me back to work thoroughly overhauled and refitted," he said to Daphne, as she displayed, not without pride, his renovated garments laid out upon the spare bed. "I feel like a cruiser coming out of dry dock."

"Well, don't get your things in that state again," said Daphne severely—"that's all! Who looks after them?"

"My man."

"He ought to be ashamed of himself, then. By the way, there is a dress waistcoat of yours with two buttons off. Can I *trust* you, now, to get them put on again, or had I better keep the waistcoat until I can get buttons to match?"

"You are very good," said Juggernaut, bowing before the storm.

"That's settled, then. Where shall I send it to?"

Juggernaut thought, and finally gave the address of a club in Pall Mall.

"Club—do you live in a *club*?" inquired Daphne, with a woman's instinctive dislike for such a monastic and impregnable type of domicile.

"Sometimes. It saves trouble, you see," said Juggernaut apologetically. "My house in town is shut at present. I spend a good deal of time in the north."

"Where do you live when you are in the north?" inquired Daphne, with the healthy curiosity of her age and sex.

"I have another house there," admitted Juggernaut reluctantly. "It is called Belton."

"How many houses have you got altogether?" asked Daphne, in the persuasive tones of a schoolmaster urging a reticent culprit to make a clean breast of it and get it over like a man.

"I have a little place in the Highlands," said Juggernaut humbly—

Daphne rolled her brown eyes up to the ceiling.

—"But it is the merest shooting-box," he added, as if pleading for a light sentence.

"Is that all?"

"Yes—on my honour!"

"And—you live in a *club*!"

Then came the verdict—the inevitable verdict.

"What you want," said Daphne, regarding the impassive features of the prisoner at the bar, "is a wife. It's not too late, really," she added, smiling kindly upon him. "Of course, you think now at your age that you could never get used to it, but you could."

"Do you think any girl would marry a man practically in his dotage?" inquired Juggernaut respectfully.

"Not a girl, perhaps," admitted Daphne, "but somebody sensible and good. I'll tell you what—don't you know any nice widows? A widow would suit you top-hole. She would be used to men already, which would help her a lot, poor thing! Then, she would probably let you down more easily than an old maid. She would know, for instance, that it's perfectly hopeless to get a man to keep his room tidy, or to stop leaving his slippers about on the dining-room hearthrug, or dropping matches and ash on the floor. Do marry a widow, Sir John! Don't you know of any?"

Sir John smiled grimly.

"I will consult my visiting-list," he said; "but I won't promise anything. In spite of the apparent docility of my character, there are just one or two things which I prefer to do in my own way."

"Still, I don't despair of you," said Daphne. "Old Martin down in the village married only the other day, and he was seventy-two. Nearly bedridden, in fact," she added encouragingly.

That evening after supper the Rectory children sat round the table engaged in card games of a heating and complicated nature, Miss Vereker as usual doubling the parts of croupier and referee. The guest and the Rector were smoking in the study.

Suddenly the door of the dining-room opened, and Brian Vereker appeared.

"Daphne, my daughter," he said, "can you leave these desperadoes for a while and join us in the study?"

"All right, Dad. Ally, you had better be dealer. Nicky, if you cheat while I am away you know the penalty! Come with me, Dawks. So long, everybody. Back directly!"

But she was wrong. Game succeeded game: the time slipped by unheeded by all except Nicky and Tony, who, because it was past their hour for going to bed, noted its flight with special and personal relish; and it was not until the almost tearful Cilly had been rendered an old maid for the fourth consecutive time that the family realised that it was nearly half-past ten and Daphne had not returned.

"Of course," said Nicky, wagging her head triumphantly, "we all know what *that* means!"

And for once in her small, scheming, prying life, she was right.

CHAPTER SEVEN.

THE MATCH IS STRUCK.

Daphne sat rather dizzily by her father's side, holding his hand tightly and gazing straight before her. A sudden turn, and lo! before her lay a great break in the road. She had arrived at one of life's jumping-off places. No wonder she gripped her father's hand.

Now, for a young girl to consent to a marriage with a man considerably older than herself, a man whom she hardly knows and does not love, is rightly regarded as a most unromantic proceeding; and since romance is the sugar of this rather acrid existence of ours, we are almost unanimous in discouraging such alliances. And yet there are two sides to the question. A loveless marriage may lead to the ruin of two lives: on the other hand, it introduces into the proceedings an element of business and common-sense all too rare in such enterprises. It is true that the newly united pair dream no dreams and see no visions. Each comes to the other devoid of glamour or false pretences. But if a couple find marriage feasible under such circumstances, the chances are that they are of a type which stands in no need of that highly intoxicating stimulant, Passion. They are simply people who realise at the outset, instead of later on, that life is a campaign and not a picnic; and each sees in the other not so much an idol or a plaything as a trusty ally. For such, mutual respect cannot but spring into being, and will in all likelihood grow into mutual love; and mutual love which matures from such beginnings as these is ten thousand times more to be desired than the frothy headachy stuff which we quaff in such reckless magnums in our thirsty youth.

On the other hand, marriages made on earth (as opposed to what are popularly regarded as the celestial variety) can and often do lead to shipwreck. Granted. Still, marriage is a leap in the dark in any case, and humdrum philosophers must at least be excused for suggesting that one may as well endeavour to illuminate this hazardous feat of agility by the help of the Torch of Reason as not. But of course no one ever agrees with such suggestions. Romance and Sentiment cry, "Never! Shame! Monstrous!" And most of us very humanly, naturally, and rightly associate ourselves in the most cordial manner with the opinions of this old-established and orthodox firm.

We left Daphne gazing into the study fire, with a silent man on either side of her and Mr Dawks' head upon her knee. She looked perfectly composed, but something was rocking and trembling within her.

It is certainly disconcerting, even for the most self-possessed of maidens, to realise, suddenly and without warning, that there are deeper things than the domestic affections. It is still more disconcerting when an individual whom Nature might with perfect propriety have appointed your father, and whom you with feminine perversity have adopted as a son, suddenly kicks over the traces and suggests as a compromise that he should occupy the intermediate position of husband.

Brian Vereker sat smiling, happy and confident. The fact that Sir John Carr was forty-two and Daphne barely twenty had not occurred to him. All he realised was that the little boy who had been his fag at school, who had lit his fire and made his toast in return for occasional help with cæsuras and quadratic equations, had grown up into a man, and desired to marry his daughter. The whole thing seemed so natural, so appropriate. He glowed with humble pride that Providence should so interest itself in his little household. He beamed upon the young people.

Suddenly Daphne turned to him, and released her hold on his hand.

"Dad, will you leave us for a little?" she said. "I want to talk to Sir John."

The Rector rose.

"By all means," he said. "Now I come to think of it, the presence of a third party is not essential to a proposal of marriage. I am *de trop*! I shall be upstairs."

He laughed boyishly, and left them.

When the door closed Daphne turned to her suitor.

"So you want me for your wife?" she said, with the air of one opening a debate.

"I do," said Juggernaut. It was the first time he had spoken since she entered the room.

"And you went and saw Dad about it," continued Daphne, rather unexpectedly.

"Yes. As I understood you were not of age, I asked his permission to speak to you. He rather took the words out of my mouth by calling you in and telling you himself."

"I'm glad to hear you say that," said Daphne. "I thought at first the thing was being arranged over my head, and that I wasn't to be consulted at all.

But you *were* going to ask me properly, weren't you? We prefer that, you know." She spoke for her sex.

Juggernaut nodded.

"Only Dad rushed in and spoiled it—eh?"

"That is correct," said Juggernaut.

"Well, begin now," said Daphne calmly. "A girl doesn't like to be done out of a proposal. It would be something to tell the kids about afterwards, anyhow."

Juggernaut became conscious of a distinctly more lenient attitude towards the Rector's precipitancy.

"Now that you know," he began, "a formal proposal would sound rather dull and superfluous, wouldn't it?"

"Perhaps you are right," said Daphne, half regretfully. "Dad has spoiled it for me, after all!"

Presently—

"I wonder *why* you want to marry me," she mused, fondling Mr Dawks' ears. "I suppose you have come to the conclusion that it is time you had some one to look after all those houses and servants of yours. Is that it?"

Juggernaut regarded her curiously for a moment.

"Perhaps," he said.

"You are not in love with me, of course," continued the practical Miss Vereker, ticking off the unassailable features of the case. "At least, I suppose not—I don't see how you possibly could be. It's rather hard for me to tell, though, because I don't quite know the meaning of the word. I love Dad and the boys, and Cilly, and Nicky, and Mr Dawks—*don't* I, Dawks, dear?—and I would do *anything* to save them pain or unhappiness. But I suppose that's not the sort of love that people call love. It seems to have been left out of my composition, or perhaps it hasn't cropped up yet. Now Cilly—I am her exact opposite—Cilly is always in love with some man or other. By the way, she told me last night when I went to dry her hair that she had just fallen in love with you, so evidently you aren't too old after all! Would it do as well if you married Cilly?" Daphne inquired tentatively.

"I'm afraid not," said Juggernaut.

"Well, perhaps you are right. Cilly's a darling, but she is very young yet," agreed the time-worn Miss Vereker. "But"—she broke off short—"it seems to me that I am doing most of the talking. Would you care to address the meeting—say a few words? I think I should like to hear a bit of that proposal after all. So far, all I know is that you want to marry me. And *that* I got from Dad. Now—I'm listening!"

Daphne leaned back in her big chair and smiled upon her suitor quite maternally. There was something pathetic in her childish freedom from embarrassment or constraint under circumstances which usually test the *sang-froid* of man and maid alike. Perhaps Sir John was struck by this, for his eyes suddenly softened and the lines about his mouth relaxed.

"You needn't say you love me, or anything like that, if you don't," supplemented Daphne. "I shall understand."

Sir John's eyes resumed their normal appearance.

"As you seem to prefer to keep matters on a strictly business footing," he said, "I will come to the point at once. If you will marry me I think I can make you tolerably happy and comfortable. I am a prosperous man, I suppose, and as my wife you would find a certain social position awaiting you. Any desires of yours in the way of houses, clothes, jewels, and so on, you could always gratify, within limits, at will. I mention these things, not because I think they will influence your decision—I should not want you for a wife if I thought they would—but because I feel that every woman is entitled to a plain statement of fact about the man who wishes to marry her. Too often, under the delusion that the sheer romance of a love-affair wipes all mundane considerations off the slate, she puts up with the wildest of fictions. However, I may point out to you that acceptance of my worldly goods would enable you to carry out certain schemes that I know lie very near your heart. You could send Ally to the University. You could have Cilly finished, or whatever the expression is, and bring her out yourself. And you could pay for a curate for your father. You can have all the money you want for these enterprises by asking for it; or if you prefer something more definite I would settle an annual sum upon you—say a thousand a-year."

A thousand a-year! Daphne closed her eyes giddily. Before her arose a vision of a renovated Rectory—a sort of dimity Palace Beautiful—with an enlarged kitchen-boiler, new carpets, and an extra servant. She saw her father bending happily over his sermon while a muscular young Christian tramped round the parish. She saw Ally winning first classes at Cambridge, and Cilly taking London drawing-rooms by storm. Her pulse quickened. But Juggernaut was still speaking.

"On the other hand, I ought to warn you that I am a hard man—at least, I believe that is my reputation—with somewhat rigid notions on the subject of *quid* and *quo*. I would endeavour to supply my wife with every adjunct to her happiness; but—I should expect her in return to stand by my side and do her duty as my wife so long as we both lived. They say of me that I never make a mistake in choosing a lieutenant. Well, the instinct which has served me so often in that respect is prompting me now; and it is because I see in you a woman who would stand by her husband as a matter of duty alone, quite apart from"—he hesitated—"from inclination, that I ask you to marry me."

Daphne gazed at him. Her heart was bumping gently. There was something rather fine about this proposed bargain—a compact between a man and a woman to stand by one another through thick and thin, not because they liked doing so but because it was playing the game. Daphne felt proud, too, that this master of men should have adjudged her—a woman—to be of the true metal. But she was honest to the end.

"You would give all that to have me for your wife," she said.

Sir John bowed his head with grave courtesy.

"I would," he said simply.

"I'm not worth it," said Daphne earnestly. "I am only accustomed to looking after our little Rectory and the family. I might make a fearful mess of all your grand houses. Supposing I did? What if I wasn't up to your mark? How if your friends didn't like me? It would be too late to send me back," she pointed out, rather piteously.

Sir John's features did not relax.

"I am willing to take the risk," was all he said.

There was a long pause.

"Let me think," said Daphne suddenly and feverishly.

She slipped out of her chair on to the hearthrug, and lay before the twinkling fire with her arms clasped round the neck of the ever-faithful Mr Dawks and her face buried in his rough coat. There was a tense silence, accentuated by the amiable thumping of Dawks' tail. Sir John Carr sat in his chair like a graven image, looking down upon the slim lithe figure at his feet. Daphne just then was a sight to quicken the blood in a man's veins, but Juggernaut never moved. Perhaps he realised, for all his lack of lover's graces and his harsh methods of wooing, something of the solemnity of the moment. A child, without experience, with nothing but her own untutored instincts to guide her, was standing at her cross-roads. Would she go forward with the man whose path through life had so suddenly converged on hers, or fare on alone? And the man—what were his feelings? None could have told by outward view. He simply waited—sitting very still.

At last Daphne sat up, and shook back her hair from her eyes.

"We'll leave it to Mr Dawks," she said. "Dawks, old boy, shall we *do* it?"

The house waited in breathless silence for Mr Dawks' casting vote. That affectionate and responsive arbitrator, hearing himself addressed, raised his head, licked his mistress's hand, and belaboured the floor with his tail in a perfect ecstasy of cordiality.

Daphne turned to the man in the chair.

"All right!" she said. "It's a bargain. I'll marry you."

CHAPTER EIGHT.

"MORITURA TE SALUTAT."

On a bright spring afternoon three weeks later the Rectory children sat huddled together like a cluster of disconsolate starlings upon the five-barred gate leading into Farmer Preston's big pasture meadow.

It was the eve of Daphne's wedding-day.

To those readers of this narrative who feel inclined to dilate upon the impropriety of marrying in haste, it may be pointed out that the bride possessed no money and the bridegroom no relatives. Consequently there would be no presents, no *trousseau*. The principal incentives to what Miss Veronica Vereker pithily described as a "circus wedding" being thus eliminated, the pair were to be married quietly next day in the little church where Daphne had been christened and confirmed, and under the shadow of which she had lived all her short life.

As noted above, the bride had no *trousseau*, for her father could not afford one, and she flatly declined to take a penny from her *fiancé* until he became her husband. The little village dressmaker had turned out a wedding-dress over which Cilly hourly gloated, divided between ecstasy and envy; and this, together with an old lace veil in which her mother had been married, would serve Daphne's needs.

In truth, she had little time to think of herself. She was relinquishing a throne which she had occupied since she was eleven years old, and the instruction and admonition of her successor had occupied her attention ever since the date of her wedding had been fixed. Keys had to be handed over, recipes confided, and the mysteries of feminine book-keeping unfolded. There were good-byes to be said to bedridden old women and tearful cottage children. The bridegroom too, she felt, had a certain claim upon her attention. He had departed the morning after Daphne had accepted him, and was now very busy preparing his house in London for the reception of the future Lady Carr. But he had spent a good deal of time at the Rectory for all that, coming down for week-ends and the like; and Daphne, mindful of the duties of a *fiancée*, devoted herself conscientiously to his entertainment whenever he appeared.

But now the end of all things was imminent. To-morrow the management of the Rectory would pass into the hands of the dubious and inexperienced Cilly.

Meanwhile the Rectory children continued to sit disconsolately upon the gate. They were waiting for Daphne, who had promised to spend her last afternoon with them. Sir John, who was now staying at Kirkley Abbey,—to the mingled apprehension and exhilaration of the chief bridesmaid Lord Kirkley had offered to act as best man,—was to come over that afternoon, but only to see the Rector on matters connected with settlements and other unromantic adjuncts to the married state.

The gate proving unsuitable for prolonged session, the family abandoned their gregarious attitude and disposed of themselves in more comfortable fashion. Ally, home on two days' special leave from school, lay basking in the sun. Cilly sprawled on the grass with her back against a tree trunk, her brow puckered with the gradual realisation of coming responsibility. Stiffy, simple soul, with his knees clasped beneath his chin, sorrowfully contemplated to-morrow's bereavement. Master Anthony Cuthbert, perched on a log with a switch in his hand, was conducting an unseen orchestra. Nicky, soulless and flippant as ever, speculated at large upon her sister's future.

"It'll be pretty hot for Daph living down there at first," she mused. A joke lasted Nicky a long time: the humorous fiction that the bride-elect would to-morrow be carried off to reside permanently in the infernal regions was still as a savoury bakemeat to her palate. "Of course, Polly"—this was her abbreviation for Apollyon, adopted as soon as that gentleman had ascended from the grade of familiar friend to that of prospective relative—"will be glad to get back to his own fireside, but Daph will feel it a bit, I should think. Perhaps he will let her use a screen to begin with!... I wonder what housekeeping will be like. I suppose the cook will have horns and a tail, and all the food will be devilled. I should like to see Daph ordering dinner. 'Good morning, Diabolo!' 'Good morning, miss! What would you like for dinner to-night?' 'Well, Diabolo, what have you *got*?' 'There's a nice tender sinner came in this morning, miss. You might have a few of his ribs; or would you prefer him served up grilled, with brimstone sauce? And I suppose you would like devils-on-horseback for a savoury.' 'That will do *very* nicely, Diabolo. Oh, I forgot! It's possible that the Lucifers will drop in. Perhaps we'd better have yesterday's moneylender cold on the side-board in case there isn't enough to go round. And we must have something special to'—Ally, what do people drink in Hades?"

"Dunno," said Ally drowsily; "molten lead, I should think."

"Only the *lower* classes, dear," said Nicky witheringly. "I am talking about the best people."

"Sulphuric acid?" suggested Ally, who was beginning to study chemistry at school.

"That will do," said Nicky, and returned to her dialogue. "'Diabolo, will you tell the butler to put a barrel—no, a *vat*—of sulphuric acid on ice. You know what the Lucifers are, when'—hallo, here's Daph at last!"

The bride-elect approached, swinging her garden-hat in her hand, and followed by Mr Dawks.

"Well, family," she said, "I'm yours for the rest of the day. What shall we do?"

"Where is John?" inquired Ally. (John, it may be explained, was the name by which the family, with the exception of Nicky, had decided to address their future brother-in-law.)

"In the study with Dad."

"Has he arranged about having the five o'clock train stopped to-morrow afternoon?" inquired the careful Stiffy.

"No. We are going in a motor all the way to London," said Daphne. "Jack was keeping it as a surprise for me. It's a new one, a———"

"All the way to *where*?" inquired that economical humourist, Miss Veronica Vereker.

"London."

"H'm! Yes, I *have* heard it called that, now I come to think of it," conceded Nicky; "but it seems a waste of a good car, especially if it's a new one. Unless it's made of some special—Stiffy, what's the name of that stuff that won't burn?"

"Asbestos?"

"That's it—asbestos. I didn't expect to see you drive off down the road, somehow," continued Nicky in a somewhat injured voice, "just like an ordinary couple. I thought Polly would stamp his foot on the lawn, and a chasm would yawn at your feet, and in you'd both pop, and you would be gone for ever, like—Ally, who were those two people in the Latin book you had for a holiday task?"

"What you want, Nicky," responded Mr Aloysuis Vereker, "is chloroform. Do you mean Pluto and Proserpine?"

"That's it—Proserpine. Well, Proserpine, what are you going to do to entertain your little brothers and sisters this afternoon?"

"Anything you like," said Proserpine, endeavouring to balance herself on the top bar of the gate. "How about making toffee down in the Den?"

There was a chorus of approval. Nursery customs die hard. Even the magnificent Ally found it difficult to shake off the glamour of this youthful dissipation.

"I'll tell you what," continued Daphne, warming up to the occasion, "we'll have a regular farewell feast. We'll send down to the shop and get some buns and chocolates and gingerbeer, and—and———"

"Bananas," suggested Tony.

"Nuts," added Cilly.

"Cigarettes," said Ally.

"Who has got any money?" inquired Nicky.

The family fumbled in its pockets.

"Here's threepence—all I have," said Cilly at length.

"Twopence," said Ally, laying the sum on Cilly's threepenny bit.

"Awfully sorry," said Stiffy, "but I'm afraid I've only got a stamp. It's still quite gummy at the back, though," he added hopefully. "They'll take it."

Tony produced a halfpenny.

"You can search *me*, friends!" was Nick's despairing contribution.

"I have fourpence," said the bride—"not a penny more. I handed over all the spare housekeeping money to Dad this morning. That only makes tenpence-halfpenny, counting Stiffy's stamp." She sighed wistfully. "And I did so want to give you all a treat before I went! Well, we must do without the nuts and chocolates, and———"

Nicky rose to her feet, swelling with sudden inspiration.

"Daph, what's the matter with running along to this millionaire young man of yours and touching *him* for a trifle?" she inquired triumphantly.

Daphne hesitated. True, to-morrow she would be a rich man's wife, able to afford unlimited gingerbeer. But the idea of asking a man for money did not appeal to her. Pride of poverty and maidenly reserve make an obstinate mixture. Yet the flushed and eager faces of Nicky and Tony, the polite deprecations of the selfless Stiffy, and the studied indifference of Cilly and Ally, were hard to resist.

"I wonder if he would mind," she said doubtfully.

"Mind? Oh, no. Why should he?" urged the chorus respectfully.

"Have a dart for it, anyhow," said Nicky.

Daphne descended from the gate.

"Righto!" she said. "After all, it's our last afternoon together, and I *should* like to do you all proud. I'll chance it. The rest of you can start down to the Den and collect sticks, while I run along to the house and ask him. Nicky, you had better come with me to carry down saucepans and things. Come on—I'll race you!"

Three minutes later, Sir John Carr, smoking a meditative cigar upon the lawn, was aware of a sudden scurry and patter in the lane outside. Directly after this, with a triumphant shriek, the small figure of his future sister-in-law shot through the garden-gate, closely followed by that of his future wife. Mr Dawks, faint yet pursuing, brought up the rear.

The competitors flung themselves down on the grass at his feet, panting.

"We have been having a race," explained Daphne rather gratuitously.

"I won!" gasped Nicky. "Daph has the longest legs," she continued, "but I have the shortest skirts. Now, my children, I must leave you. Wire in!" she concluded, in a hoarse and penetrating whisper to Daphne.

Her short skirts flickered round the corner of the house, and she was gone. Daphne was left facing her *fiancé*.

"I say," she began rather constrainedly—"don't get up; I'm not going to stay—do you think you could lend me a little money? I—I'll pay you back in a day or two," she added with a disarming smile. "The fact is, we are going to make toffee down in the Den, and I wanted to get a few extra things, just to give them all a real treat to finish up with, you know. Will you—Jack?"

Juggernaut looked up at her with his slow scrutinising smile.

"What sort of extra things?" he inquired.

"Oh!"—Daphne closed her eyes and began to count on her fingers— "buns, and chocolates, and nuts, and gingerbeer. And I wanted to give Ally a packet of cigarettes. (After all, he's eighteen, and he does love them so, and they are only ten for threepence.) And if you could run to it, I should like to get a few bananas as well," she concluded with a rush, laying all her cards on the table at once.

Juggernaut leaned back in his chair and looked extremely judicial.

"What will all this cost?" he inquired.

"One and eleven," said Daphne. "Jack, you *dear*! We *shall* have a time!"

Juggernaut had taken a handful of change out of his pocket.

"One and eleven," he said; "I wonder, Daphne, if you will be able to purchase an afternoon of perfect happiness for that sum in a year's time."

He handed over the money.

"May I have a receipt?" he asked gravely.

Daphne took his meaning, and kissed him lightly. She lingered for a moment, anxious not to appear in a hurry to run away.

"Is there anything else?" inquired Sir John at length.

Daphne ran an inward eye over the possibilities of dissipation.

"No, I don't think so," she said. "Thanks ever so much! We shall be back about six. So long, old man. Don't go to sleep in this hot sun."

She flitted away across the lawn, jingling the money in her hand. At the gate she turned and waved her hand. Juggernaut's eyes were fixed upon her, but he did not appear to observe her salutation. Probably he was in a brown study about something.

Daphne was half-way down to the Den before it occurred to her that it would have been a graceful act—not to say the barest civility—to invite the donor of the feast to come and be present thereat. But she did not go back.

"It would bore him so, poor dear!" she said to herself; "and—and us, too!"

Next day they were married.

BOOK TWO.

FLICKERINGS.

CHAPTER NINE.

A HORSE TO THE WATER.

"And how is her ladyship?" inquired Mrs Carfrae.

"Her ladyship," replied Sir John Carr, "is enjoying life. What good bread-and-butter you always keep."

They were sitting in Mrs Carfrae's tiny drawing-room in Hill Street. Mrs Carfrae was a little old lady in a wheeled chair. Her face was comparatively youthful, but her hair was snowy white. She spoke with what English people, to whom the pure Highland Scots of Inverness and the guttural raucousness of Glasgow are as one, term "a Scotch accent."

"I am glad you like my bread-and-butter," she said; "but I fancy you get as good at your wife's tea-table."

"I don't often see my wife's tea-table," confessed Juggernaut. "She is out a good deal, and as a rule it is more convenient for me to have my tea sent into my study."

"Where you grumble at it, I'll be bound. I ken husbands. So her ladyship is out a good deal? Well do I mind the first time I caught her in, the besom! That was nearly three years ago. I am not a payer of calls, as you know; but I felt that I must be the very first to greet your wife, Johnny boy. So the day after I knew you had settled in, I had myself bundled into the carriage, and off I went to Grosvenor Street. I told Maxwell to ring the bell and inquire if her ladyship was at home. The door was thrown open immediately—rather prematurely, in fact. I heard a sound like the cheep of a frightened mouse, and I saw a grand silk skirt and a pair of ankles scuttering up the staircase. I knew fine what had happened. I was her first caller: and though the child was sitting in her new drawing-room waiting for me and those like me, her courage had failed at the sound of the bell, and she was galloping up the stair out of the way when the man opened the door. Poor lassie! I did exactly the same thing at her age."

"Did you go in?"

"I did. I was determined to do it. I gripped my crutch and was out of the carriage and up the steps before the footman could answer Maxwell. I hobbled past the man—he just gaped at me like a puddock on a hot day—and got to the foot of the stair and looked up. As I expected, there was Madam, hanging over the banisters to see what sort of a caller she had hooked the first time. There was another creature beside her, with wild brown hair and eyes like saucers. They were clutching each other round the waist. When they saw me they gave a kind of horrified yelp. But I cried to them to come down, and in ten minutes we were the best of friends. They were terribly prim at first; but when they found out that I was just a clavering old wife and nothing more, they lost their grand manners. They overlaid me with questions about London, and while I was answering them the saucer-eyed one set to work cracking lumps of sugar with her teeth. The other—her ladyship—was eating jam out of an Apostle spoon. The spoon was in her mouth when a footman came in to mend the fire. She was fairly taken by surprise, and tried to push the whole concern into her mouth until the man should be gone. I thought at first she had swallowed it, but presently I saw the Apostle sticking out. And that was three years ago. Well, I have become less active since then, and I pay no more calls—wheel me a piece nearer the fire, Johnny—so I do not see so much of her ladyship as I did. Still, I am glad to hear she is enjoying life. And how is the baby?"

"The baby," replied its male parent, "looks and sounds extremely robust. He uttered several articulate words the other day, I am told."

"Can he walk?"

"He can lurch along in a slightly dissipated manner."

"Good! And how does your Daphne handle all these houses and servants of yours?"

Sir John smiled.

"She was a little out of her depth at first," he said. "She had not been accustomed to cater for a large household. The extravagance of ordering at least one fresh joint a-day appalled her, and it was a long time before the housekeeper could cure her of a passion for shepherd's pie. But she has a shrewd head. She soon discovered which items of domestic expenditure were reasonable and which were not. She has cut down the bills by a half, but I don't notice any corresponding falling off in the quality of the *menu*."

"And does she love fine clothes, and gaiety?"

"I think she found her maid rather a trial at first. She had been so accustomed not only to attiring herself but to going round and hooking up her sisters as well, that a woman who handled her like a baby rather paralysed her. She also exhibited a *penchant* for wearing her old clothes out—to rags, that is—in private. But I think she is getting over that now. I received her dressmaker's latest bill this morning. It reveals distinct signs of progress."

"And I hear she looks just beautiful."

"She does. I must admit that."

"*Then*," the old lady raised herself a little in her chair, and settled her spectacles with her unparalysed hand, "what is the trouble, Johnny Carr?"

Juggernaut laid down his tea-cup with a slight clatter.

"I was not aware," he said curtly, "that there was any trouble."

Mrs Carfrae surveyed him long and balefully over her spectacles.

"Johnny Carr," she observed dispassionately, "I have known you ever since you could roar for your bottle, and I have never had any patience with you either then or since. You are a dour, dreich, thrawn, camstearie creature. You have more money than you can spend, grand health, and a young and beautiful wife. But you are not happy. You come here to tell me so, and when I ask you to begin, you say there is nothing! Well, *I* will tell you what the matter is. There is some trouble between you and your Daphne."

Considerable courage is required to inform a man to his face that all is not well between him and his wife; but courage was a virtue that Elspeth Carfrae had never lacked. Juggernaut experienced no feeling of resentment or surprise that this old lady should have instantaneously sized up a situation which he himself had been investigating in a groping and uncertain fashion for nearly three years. Life is a big book of problems, and while man is content to work them out figure by figure, taking nothing for granted which cannot be approved by established formulæ, woman has an exasperating habit of skipping straight to the solution in a manner which causes the conscientious and methodical male to suspect her of peeping at the answers at the end of the book.

"Perhaps you had not realised that," pursued Mrs Carfrae. "Men are apt to be slow in the uptake," she added indulgently.

"I fail to see where you get your *data* from," replied Juggernaut. "I have not been particularly communicative on the subject. In fact, I don't remember telling you a single——"

Mrs Carfrae subjected him to a withering glare.

"If all that women knew," she observed frostily, "was what men had told them, I wonder how many of us would be able to spell our own names. No, laddie, you have told me nothing: that's true enough. But I know fine why you came here to-day. You are worried. You and Daphne are getting on splendidly. The match has been a great success. You have a son and heir. But—you are not happy; and it is about your Daphne that you are not happy."

Juggernaut gazed into the fire.

"You are right," he said. "I confess that my marriage has not been so uplifting as I had hoped. I daresay it is my own fault. As you point out, I am—well, all the Caledonian adjectives you heaped upon me just now: all that and a good deal more. I have the reputation of being a harsh man, and I hate it. I hoped, when I married that child, that she would pull me out of my rigid, undeviating way of life, and broaden my sympathies a little. I looked forward to a little domesticity." His dark face coloured slightly. "I may be an ogre, but I have my soft side, as you know."

"None better," said the old lady gently.

"Well, somehow," continued Juggernaut, "my marriage has not made the difference to me that I had hoped. We two have had our happy hours together, but we don't seem to progress beyond a certain point. We are amiability itself. If I ask Daphne to see to anything about the house, she sees to it; if she asks me to go with her to a tea-fight, I go. But that seems to be about the limit. I can't help thinking that marriage would not have survived so long as an institution if there had been no more behind it than that. I was under the impression that it made two one. At present we are still two—very decidedly two; and—and——"

"And being you, it just maddens you not to be able to get your money's worth," said Mrs Carfrae calmly. "Now, John Carr, just listen to me. First of all, have you had any trouble with her?"

"Trouble?"

"Yes. Any direct disagreement with her?"

"Never. Stop—we had one small breeze."

Mrs Carfrae wagged a forefinger.

"You have been bullying her, monster!"

"Heavens, no!"

"Well, tell me the story."

"Six months ago," said Juggernaut, "she came to me and asked for money—much as a child asks for toffee—with a seraphic smile and an ingratiating rub up against my chair. I asked her what it was for."

"Quite wrong!" said Mrs Carfrae promptly.

"But surely——" began Juggernaut, the man of business up in arms at once.

"You should have begun by taking out your cheque-book and saying, 'how much?'" continued his admonitress. "Then she would have called you a dear, or some such English term of affection, and recognising you as her natural confidant would have told you everything. After that you might have improved the occasion. As it was, you just put her back up, and she dithered."

"She did, so far as I understand the expression. But, finding that I was firm——"

"Oh, man, man, how can a great grown creature like you bear to be *firm— hard*, you mean, of course—with a wild unbroken lass like that? Well, go on. You were firm. And what did her poor ladyship say she wanted the money for?"

"For her young cub of a brother," said Juggernaut briefly.

"A wealthy young wife daring to want to help her own brother! Monstrous!" observed Mrs Carfrae.

"I think you are unjust to me in this matter. Listen! When I married Daphne I was aware that she would want to finance her entire family: in fact, it was one of the inducements to marrying me which I laid before her. For that purpose, to save her the embarrassment of constantly coming to me for supplies, I settled upon her a private allowance of—what do you think?"

"Out with it! No striving after effect with *me*, my man!" was the reply of his unimpressionable audience.

"I gave her a thousand a year," said Juggernaut.

"That should have been sufficient," said Mrs Carfrae composedly. "But do not be ostentatious about it. You could well afford the money."

"Well, she had spent most of that year's allowance in six months," continued Juggernaut, disregarding these gibes—"on her father's curate, the younger children's education, and so forth—and she wanted more."

"What age is this brother?"

"Twenty, I think. He is up at Cambridge, and wants to get into the Army as a University candidate. At present he appears to be filling in his time philandering with a tobacconist's daughter. The tobacconist's bill for moral and intellectual damage came to five hundred pounds. Before writing the cheque, I stipulated—"

"You would!" said the old lady grimly.

—"That I should be permitted to make a few investigations on my own behalf. Young Vereker is a handsome, fascinating rascal, with about as much moral fibre as a Yahoo. He was a good deal franker in his admissions to me than he had been to his sister—"

"Ay, I once heard you cross-examining a body," confirmed Mrs Carfrae.

—"And on the completion of my inquiries I paid the money down on the nail. It was the only thing to do."

"Did you tell Daphne the whole story?"

"No. I should hate to dispel her illusions. She loves her brothers and sisters."

"There is no need to excuse yourself, John Carr. I knew fine that you would not tell her. Instead, you glowered at her, and read her a lecture about extravagance and improvidence. She tried to look prim and penitent, but danced down the stair the moment she got the door shut behind her. Now, mannie, listen to me. This is no light charge you have taken on yourself—to rule a wild, shy, impulsive taupie like that. You cannot contain the like with bit and bridle, mind. I have been one myself, and I know. There is just one thing to do. She must learn to *love* you, or the lives of the pair of you will go stramash!"

Juggernaut's old friend concluded this homily with tremendous emphasis, and there was a long silence. Then the man drew his chair a little closer.

"How can I teach her?" he asked humbly. "I have no *finesse*, no attractiveness. Do you think I—I am too old for her?"

"Old? Toots! I was nineteen when I married on my Andy, and he was thirty-nine. For the first few years after we married I called him 'daddy' to his face. After that I found that I was really old enough to be the man's mother; so I called him 'sonny.' But that is a digression. I will tell you how to teach her. Do not be monotonous. It's no use just to be a good husband to her: any gowk can be that. Do not let your affection run on in a regular, dutiful stream: have a spate occasionally! Get whirled off your feet by her, and let her see it. Prepare some unexpected ploy for her. Rush her off to dine somewhere on the spur of the moment—just your two selves. Stop her suddenly on the staircase in a half-light, and give her a hug."

"She'd never stand it!" cried Juggernaut in dismay. "And I could never do it," he added apprehensively.

"You *do* it, my callant," said Mrs Carfrae with decision, "and she'll stand it right enough! She may tell you not to be foolish, but she will not make a point of coming down by the back stair in future for all that. And let her see that with you she comes *first* in everything. What a crow she will have to herself when she realises that a feckless unbusinesslike piece like herself has crept right into the inmost place in the heart of a man whose gods used to be hard work and hard words and hard knocks! She'll just glory in you!

"Lastly, do not be discouraged if you have no success to begin with. At all costs you must keep on smiling. A dour, bleak man is no fit companion for a young girl who has always lived a sheltered sunny life. He just withers her. She may last for a while, and do her duty by him, but in time he'll break her heart. Ay, keep on smiling, Johnny, even if she hurts you. She will hurt you often. Young girls are like that. It takes time for a woman to realise that a man is just about twice as sensitive as herself in certain matters, and she will not make allowances for him at first. But until she does—and she will, if you give her time—keep on smiling! If you keep on long enough you will get your reward. Make the effort, my man! I have had to make efforts in my time—"

"I know that," said Juggernaut.

—"And the efforts have been the making of *me*. For one thing, I have acquired a sense of proportion. When we are young and lusty our knowledge of perspective is so elementary that in our picture of life our own Ego fills the foreground to the exclusion of all else; with this result, that we get no view of the countless interesting and profitable things that lie behind. My Ego is kept in better order these days, I assure you. It gets just a good comfortable place in the picture and no more. If Elspeth Carfrae stirs from that, or comes creeping too far forward so as to block out other things, she hears from me!"

"Does she always obey you?" asked Juggernaut.

"She got far beyond my control once," admitted the old lady. "I mind when my Andy went from me she swelled and swelled until she blotted out everything—earth, sea, and sky. But she has been back in her place these twenty years, and there she shall bide. There is no great selfish Ego blocking the view now when I sit and look out upon my section of the world. You have no idea how interesting it is to study your friends' troubles instead of your own, John. The beauty of it is that you need not worry over them: you just watch them—unconcernedly."

The Scots have their own notion of what constitutes an excursion into the realms of humour, and Juggernaut, knowing this, made no attempt to controvert his hostess's last statement.

"Not that I grudged my Andy," continued the old lady presently. "No wife worthy of the name could grudge her man to his country when he died as Andy died. But my only son—that was my own fault, maybe. I would not put him into the Army like his father, thinking to keep him safer that way; and he died of pneumonia at seven-and-twenty, an East End curate. Then my Lintie. But I have no need to be talking of Lintie to you, John Carr. You mind her still, Daphne or no Daphne. Then"—she indicated her paralysed shoulder—"this! But I keep on smiling. Perhaps that is why people are so kind to me. Perhaps if I did not smile they would not seek my company so freely. I suppose they see something in me, that they come and listen to me havering. When I first settled down here by myself in this little house many kind people called. I never thought to see them twice; but they come again and again. Maybe it is because English people have a notion that the Scots tongue is 'so quaint!' They seem to find something exhilarating in hearing fish called fush. Not that I call it any such thing, but they think I do. Anyhow, they come. Some of them bring their troubles with them, and go away without them. When they do that I know that it was worth while to keep a smiling face all these years. So smile yourself, Johnny Carr! And some day, when your Daphne comes and puts her head on your shoulder and tells you all that is troubling her, you will know that you have won through. And when that happens come and call me. I like to hear when my methods succeed."

"I will remember," said Juggernaut gravely. "Good-bye."

Mrs Carfrae watched his broad back through the doorway.

"But I doubt you will both have to be worse before you are better," she added to herself.

An hour later Lady Carr, a radiant vision of glinting hair and rustling skirts, on her way upstairs to dress for dinner, encountered her husband coming down. There was a half light. Sir John paused.

"Are you dining anywhere to-night, Daphne?" he said.

Daphne, her youthful shrewdness uneradicated by three years of adult society, replied guardedly—

"Are you trying to pull my leg? If I say 'No,' will you tell me that in that case I shall be very hungry by bedtime, or something? I suppose that old chestnut has just got round to your club. Have you been electing Noah an honorary member?"

"I was about to suggest," said Juggernaut perseveringly, "that we should go and dine at the Savoy together."

Daphne dimpled into a delighted smile.

"You dear! And we might go on somewhere afterwards. What would you like me to wear?" She preened herself in anticipation.

"Oh, anything," said Juggernaut absently. He was regarding his wife in an uncertain and embarrassed fashion.

Suddenly he drew a deep breath, and took a step down towards her. Then, with equal suddenness, he turned on his heel and retired upstairs rather precipitately in the direction of his dressing-room.

It was as well that Mrs Carfrae was not present.

CHAPTER TEN.

A DAY IN THE LIFE OF A SOCIAL SUCCESS.

By nine o'clock next morning Lady Carr, becomingly arrayed, was sitting up in bed munching a hearty breakfast, and reflecting according to her habit upon yesterday's experiences and to-day's arrangements.

She had dined with her husband at the Savoy, but the meal had not been quite such a success as she had anticipated. Juggernaut had treated her with the restrained courtesy which was habitual to him; but ladies who are taken out to dinner at the Savoy, even by their husbands, usually expect something more than restrained courtesy. You must be animated on these occasions—unless of course you happen to be a newly-engaged couple, in which case the world benignantly washes its hands of you—or the evening writes itself down a failure. Juggernaut had not been animated. He had ordered a dinner which to Daphne's gratification and surprise—she had not credited him with so much observation—had consisted almost entirely of her favourite dishes. But he had not sparkled, and sparkle at the Savoy, as already intimated, is essential.

About ten o'clock he had been called away to an important division in the House, and Daphne had gone on to a party, escorted by her husband's secretary, factotum, and right-hand man, one Jim Carthew, who arrived from Grosvenor Street in answer to a telephone summons. Carthew was a new friend of Daphne's. She accumulated friends much as a honey-pot accumulates flies, but Jim Carthew counted for more than most. They had never met until five weeks ago, for Carthew had always been up north engaged on colliery business when Daphne was in London; and when Daphne was at Belton, her husband's old home near Kilchester, Carthew had been occupied by secretarial work in town. But they had known one another by name and fame ever since Daphne's marriage, and at last they had met. Daphne was not slow to understand why her husband, impatient of assistance as he usually was, had always appeared ready to heap labour and responsibility upon these youthful shoulders. Carthew was barely thirty, but he was perfectly capable of upholding and furthering his leader's interests in the great industrial north; while down south it was generally held that whenever he grew tired of devilling for Juggernaut the Party would find him a seat for the asking.

But so far Carthew seemed loth to forsake the man who had taught him all he knew. He cherished a theory, somewhat unusual in a rising man, that common decency requires of a pupil that he shall repay his master, at the end of the period of instruction, by a period of personal service.

He was a freckle-faced youth, with a frank smile of considerable latitude, and a boyish zeal for the healthy pursuits of life. He possessed brains and character, as any man must who served under Juggernaut; and like his master he was a shrewd judge of men. Of his capacity for dealing with women Daphne knew less; but she had already heard rumours—confidences exchanged over teacups and behind fans—of a certain Miss Nina Tallentyre, perhaps the acknowledged beauty of that season, at the flame of whose altar Jim Carthew was said to have singed his wings in a conspicuously reckless fashion. But all this was the merest hearsay, and Daphne was unacquainted with the lady into the bargain. Possibly it was with a view to remedying this deficiency in her circle of acquaintance that she kept Jim Carthew at her side for the space of half an hour after they reached Mrs Blankney-Pushkins' reception.

After a couple of waltzes Lady Carr expressed a desire to be fed with ices and cream buns.

Mr Carthew assented, but with less enthusiasm than before. Daphne noticed that his eye was beginning to wander.

"After that," she continued cheerfully, "we will find seats, and you shall tell me who everybody is. I am still rather a country mouse."

"I should think so!" said Carthew, reluctantly recalling his gaze from a distant corner of the refreshment-room. "I beg your pardon! You were saying?"

"Perhaps there is some one else whom you have promised to dance with, though," continued the country mouse demurely.

Carthew, whose eye had slid stealthily round once more in the direction of a supper-party in the corner, recovered himself resolutely, and made the only reply that gallantry permitted.

"That's all right, then," said Daphne. "Tell me who those people are, having supper over there. That man with the fierce black eyes—who is he? He looks wicked."

"As a matter of fact," said Carthew, resigning himself to his fate, "he is about the most commonplace bore in the room. If he takes a girl in to dinner he talks to her about the weather with the soup, the table decorations with the fish, and suffragettes with the *entrée*. About pudding-time he takes the bit between his teeth and launches out into a description of the last play he saw—usually *Charley's Aunt* or *East Lynne*. If he goes to a wedding he refers to the church as a 'sacred edifice,' and the bride and bridegroom as 'the happy couple.' When he unexpectedly encounters a friend at a sea-side watering-place, he observes that 'the world is a very small place.' At his own funeral (to which I shall send a wreath) he will sit up and thank the mourners for 'this personal tribute of affection and esteem.'"

Daphne sat regarding this exhibition of the art of conversation with some interest. She observed that Carthew's wits were wandering, and that with inherent politeness he was exercising a purely mechanical faculty to entertain her pending their return. Jim Carthew was a true Briton in that he hated revealing his deeper thoughts to the eyes of the world. But unlike the ordinary Briton who, when his feelings do get the better of him, finds himself reduced to silent and portentous gloom, he instinctively clothed his naked shrinking soul in a garment of irresponsible frivolity. The possession of this faculty is a doubtful blessing, for it deprives many a deserving sufferer of the sympathy which is his right, and which would be his could he but take the world into his confidence. But the world can never rid itself of the notion that only still waters run deep. Consequently Jim Carthew passed in the eyes of most of his friends as a kindly, light-hearted, rather soulless trifler. But Daphne was not altogether deceived. She took an instinctive interest in this young man. She interrupted his feverish monologue, and inquired—

"Tell me, who is that girl? The tall one, with fair hair and splendid black eyes."

"What is she dressed in?" asked Carthew, surveying the throng with studied diligence.

"Flame-coloured chiffon," said Daphne.

"That is a Miss Tallentyre," replied Carthew carelessly. "Do you think she is pretty?" he added, after a slightly strained pause.

"I think she is perfectly magnificent. Do you know her?"

"Er—yes."

"Will you introduce me?" asked Daphne. "I should like to know her. See, she has just sent away her partner. Take me over and leave me with her, and then you will be free to run off and find the charmer I can see you are so anxious about."

The hapless Carthew having asserted, this time with considerably more sincerity, that he had now no further thoughts of dancing, the introduction was effected. The sequel lay this morning upon Daphne's breakfast-tray, amid a heap of invitations—Daphne was in great request at present—in the form of a note, written upon thick blue paper, in a large and rather ostentatious feminine hand. It ran—

"DEAR LADY CARR,—Don't consider me a forward young person if I ask you to be an angel and come and lunch with me to-day. I know all sorts of ceremonies ought to be observed before such a climax is reached; but will you take them for granted and *come*? We had such a tiny talk last night, and I do so want to know you better. I have been dying to make your acquaintance ever since I first saw you.—Sincerely yours,

"NINA TALLENTYRE."

Daphne was not the sort of girl to take it amiss that she, a married woman of twenty-three, with a husband and baby of her own, should informally be bidden to a feast by a young person previously unknown to her, who possessed neither. In any case the last sentence would have been too much for her vanity. She scribbled a note of acceptance to Miss Tallentyre's invitation, and set about her morning toilet.

Once downstairs, she paid her regulation punctilious visit to the library, where her husband was usually to be found until twelve o'clock. She inquired in her breezy fashion after the health of the Mother of Parliaments, and expressed a hope that her spouse had come home at a reasonable hour and enjoyed a proper night's rest. She next proceeded to the orders of the day.

"Are you dining out to-night, dear?" she inquired.

"Yes, for my sins! A City dinner at six-thirty."

"You'll be bad the morn!" quoted Lady Carr.

"True for you, Daphne. Are you going anywhere?"

"No."

"Well, you had better have Carthew to dine with you, and then he can take you to the theatre afterwards. Sorry I can't manage it my—for our two selves," he added, guiltily conscious of Mrs Carfrae's recent homily.

But Daphne was quite satisfied with the arrangement, which she designated top-hole.

"Now I am off shopping," she announced. "After that I am lunching with a girl I met last night; then Hurlingham, with the Peabodys. If you are going gorging at six-thirty, I probably shan't see you again to-day; so I'll say good-night now. Pleasant dreams! I am off to play with Baby before I go out. So long!"

She presented her husband with his diurnal kiss, and departed in search of Master Brian Vereker Carr, whose domain was situated in the upper regions of the house. Here for a time the beautiful and stately consort of Sir John Carr merged into the Daphne of old—Daphne, the little mother of all the world, the inventor of new and delightful games and repairer of all damages incurred therein. Her son's rubicund and puckered countenance lightened at her approach. He permitted his latest tooth to be exhibited without remonstrance; he nodded affably, even encouragingly, over his mother's impersonation of a dying pig; and paid her the supreme compliment of howling lustily on her departure.

Master Carr never interviewed his parents simultaneously. His father's visits—not quite so constrained as one might imagine, once the supercilious nurse had been removed out of earshot—usually took place in the evening, just before dinner; but father and mother never came together. Had they done so, it is possible that this narrative might have followed a different course. A common interest, especially when it possesses its father's mouth and its mother's eyes, with a repertory of solemn but attractive tricks with its arms and legs thrown in, is apt to be a very uniting thing.

II.

Daphne duly lunched with Miss Tallentyre.

"May I call you Daphne?" the siren asked, in a voice which intimated that a request from some people is as good as a command from most. "I have taken a fancy to you; and when I do that to anybody—which isn't often—I say so. My dear, you are perfectly *lovely*! I wish I had your complexion. You don't put anything on it, do you?"

"Soap," said Daphne briefly. She was not of the sort which takes fancies readily.

Miss Tallentyre smiled lazily.

"I see you haven't got the hang of me yet," she drawled. "You are a little offended with me. Most people are at first, but they soon find that it's not really rudeness—only *me*!—and they come round. I don't go in for rouge either. Like you, I don't need it. But I have to touch up my eyebrows. They are quite tragically sandy, and my face looks perfectly insipid if I leave them as they are." She laughed again. "Have I shocked you? You see, I believe in being frank about things—don't you? Be natural—be yourself—say what you think! That is the only true motto in life, isn't it?"

Daphne agreed cautiously. She had not yet plumbed this rather peculiar young woman. It had never occurred to her, in the whole course of her frank ingenuous existence, to ask herself whether she was herself or not. Such things were too high for her. She began to feel that she had been somewhat remiss in the matter. Miss Tallentyre appeared to have made a speciality of it.

But as shrewd Daphne was soon to discern for herself, this was only pretty Nina's way. A more confirmed *poseuse* never angled for the indiscriminate admiration of mankind. Nina Tallentyre was no fool. Having observed that in order to become conspicuous in this world it is an advantage to possess marked individuality, and having none of her own beyond that conferred by her face and figure, she decided to manufacture an individuality for her herself. She accordingly selected what she considered the most suitable of the *rôles* at her disposal, rehearsed it to her satisfaction, assumed it permanently, and played it, it must be confessed, uncommonly well. Her pose was that of the blunt and candid child of nature, and her performances ranged from unblushing flattery towards those with whom she desired to stand well to undisguised rudeness towards those whom she disliked and did not think it necessary to conciliate.

Her method prospered. Whatever wise men may think or say of us, fools usually take us at our own valuation. Consequently Miss Tallentyre never lacked a majority of admirers. She set a very high price upon her friendship, too, conferring it only as an exceptional favour; and the public, which always buys on the rise, had long since rushed in and bulled Miss Tallentyre's stock—her beauty, her wit, her transparent honesty—sky high.

The luncheon was a *tête-à-tête* function, the parent-birds, as Miss Tallentyre termed them, being absent upon a country visit. Afterwards Russian cigarettes and liqueur brandy were served with the coffee. Daphne declined these manly luxuries, but her hostess took both.

"Not that I like them," she explained with a plaintive little sigh, "but it looks *chic*; and one must be *chic* or die. Besides, I am doing it to annoy one of my admirers—one of those simple-minded, early Victorian, John Bullish creatures who dislike seeing a girl smoke, or drink cognac, or go to the theatre without a chaperone. Here is his latest effusion; it will make you shriek."

She picked up a letter from a little table by her side and began to read aloud.

"'*Nina, dear child, I know you don't care for me any more,*'—

As a matter of fact I never cared for him at any time—

'*but I can't help still taking an interest in you, and all that. I must say this. On Tuesday night I saw you sitting at supper with two men at the Vallambrosa, without anybody else to keep you in countenance, sipping liqueur brandy and smoking. Well, don't—there's a dear! You simply don't know what cruel things people say about a girl who does that sort of thing in public. Of course I know that you are absolutely——'"*

But Lady Carr was on her feet, slightly flushed.

"I think I must be going now," she said. "I had no idea it was so late. I have to meet some people at Hurlingham."

"Sorry you have to rush off," said Miss Tallentyre regretfully; "we were so cosy. Isn't this letter perfectly sweet?"

Daphne, who was glowing hotly, suddenly spoke her mind.

"If an honest man," she said, "wrote me a letter like that, I don't think I should read it aloud to total strangers, even if I was mortally offended by it. It doesn't seem to me cricket. Good-bye, and thank you so much for asking me to lunch."

"*Not* altogether a successful party," mused Daphne, as a taxi-cab conveyed her to Hurlingham. "What a hateful girl! And yet, at the back of all that affectation I believe there is something. I couldn't help liking her. She certainly is very lovely, and she must have been a darling before men got hold of her and spoiled her.... I wonder if that letter was from Jim Carthew. It sounded like his blunt blundering way of doing things. Well, he is well rid of her, anyhow. Hurrah! here is Hurlingham, and there are the Peabodys! How lovely to see the trees and grass again! And the *dear* ponies!"

The country-bred girl drew a long luxurious breath, and in the fulness of her heart grossly overpaid her charioteer on alighting. Then, forgetting Miss Tallentyre and her exotic atmosphere utterly and absolutely, she plunged with all the energy of her sunny soul into the sane delights and wholesome joys afforded by green trees, summer skies, and prancing polo-ponies.

III.

Daphne concluded her day, after a joyous drive home in the cool of the evening on the box-seat of a coach, by entertaining Jim Carthew to dinner. Afterwards he was to take her to *The Yeoman of the Guard*, which was running through a revival at the Savoy Theatre. Daphne was by no means a *blasée* Londoner as yet, for much of her short married life had been spent at Belton; and the theatre was still an abiding joy to her. On the way she rattled off a list of the pieces she had seen.

"And you have never been to a Gilbert and Sullivan opera?" asked Carthew incredulously.

"No—never."

"All I can say is—cheers!"

"Why?"

"Supposing you were a benevolent person about to introduce a small boy to his first plum-pudding, you would feel as I do," replied her companion. "But wait. Here is the theatre: we are in the fourth row of stalls."

Daphne sat raptly through the first act. Once or twice her laughter rang out suddenly and spontaneously like a child's, and indulgent persons turned and smiled sympathetically upon her; but for the most part she was still and silent, revelling in Sullivan's ever-limpid music and following the scenes that passed before her with breathless attention.

When the curtain fell slowly upon the finale of the first act—the suddenly deserted stage, the bewildered Fairfax holding his fainting bride in his arms, and the black motionless figure of the executioner towering over all— Daphne drew a long and tremulous breath, and turned to her companion.

"I understand now what you meant," she said softly. "How splendid to be able to bring some one here for the first time!"

"What surprises me," said Carthew, "is that Sir John hasn't brought you here already. I know he simply loves it."

"I am usually taken to places like the Gaiety," confessed Lady Carr. "Probably Jack considers them more suited to my intellect. Hallo, here are the orchestra-men crawling out of their holes again! Good!"

Presently the curtain went up on the last act, and Jack Point introduced a selection of the Merry Jests of Hugh Ambrose, to the audible joy of the fourth row of stalls. The Assistant Tormentor and his beloved were likewise warmly received; but presently Daphne's smiles faded. Poor Jack Point's tribulations were too much for her: during the final recurrence of *I Have a Song to Sing, O!* tears came, and as the curtain fell she dabbed her eyes hurriedly with an inadequate handkerchief.

"Awfully sorry!" she murmured apologetically. "Luckily you are not the sort to laugh at me."

Carthew silently placed her wrap round her shoulders.

"Mr Carthew," said Daphne suddenly, "will you take me somewhere gay for supper? It wouldn't be awfully improper, would it? I can't go home feeling as sad as this."

"Come along!" said Carthew.

He escorted her to an establishment where the electric lights blazed bravely, a band blared forth a cacophonous cake-walk entitled (apparently) "By

Request," and the brightest and best of the *jeunesse dorée* of London mingled in sweet companionship with the haughty but hungry divinities of the musical comedy stage.

Carthew secured a table in a secluded corner, as far as possible from the band.

"Sorry to have given you the hump," he said, with his boyish smile. "Next week I will take you to *The Mikado*. No tears there! You will laugh till you cry. Rather a bull that—what?"

He persevered manfully in this strain in his endeavour to drive away impressionable Daphne's distress on Jack Point's behalf, and ultimately succeeded.

"I hope he was *dead*, not simply in a faint," was her final reference to the subject. Then she continued: "I shall take them *all* to see that lovely piece— separately. I am not sure about Nicky, though. She is just at the scoffing age just now, and I don't think I could bear it, if she——"

"Not long ago," said Carthew, "I took a girl—that sort of girl—to see *The Yeomen*."

Daphne regarded him covertly. She knew the girl.

"Well?" she said.

"I took her on purpose," continued Carthew—"to see how she——"

Daphne, deeply interested, nodded comprehendingly.

"I know," she said. "How did she take it?"

"She never stirred," said Carthew, "all through the last act. When the curtain fell, she sat on for a few moments without saying a word, and she never spoke all the time I was taking her home. When I said good-night to her, she—she said something to me. It was not much, but it showed me that she *was* the right sort after all, in spite of what people said——"

He checked himself suddenly, as if conscious that his reminiscences were becoming somewhat intimate. But Daphne nodded a serious head.

"I'm glad," she said simply. "One likes to be right about one's friends."

Carthew shot a grateful glance at her; and presently they drifted into less personal topics, mutually conscious that here, if need be, was a friend—an understanding friend.

The evening had yet one more incident in store for Daphne.

Twelve-thirty, the *Ultima Thule* of statutory indulgence—the hour at which London, thirty minutes more fortunate than Cinderella, must perforce fly home from scenes of revelry and get ready to shake the mats—was fast approaching; and the management of the restaurant began, by a respectful but pertinacious process of light-extinguishing, to apprise patrons of the fact.

As Daphne and Carthew passed through the rapidly emptying vestibule to their cab, five flushed young gentlemen, of the *genus* undergraduate-on-the-spree, suddenly converged upon the scene from the direction of the bar, locked together in a promiscuous and not altogether unprofitable embrace. They were urged from the rear by polite but inflexible menials in brass buttons.

"What ho, Daph!"

The cry emanated from the gentleman who was acting for the moment as keystone of the arch. Daphne, stepping into the cab, looked back.

"Mr Carthew," she exclaimed, "it's Ally—my brother! He must have come up from Cambridge for the day. Do go and bring him here."

She took her seat in the hansom, and Carthew went back. Presently he returned.

"I would not advise an interview," he said drily. "Your brother—well, you know the effect of London air upon an undergraduate fresh from the country! Let him come round and see you in the morning."

He gave the cabman his orders, and their equipage drove off, just as Sebastian Aloysius Vereker, the nucleus of a gyrating mass of humanity (composed of himself and party, together with two stalwart myrmidons of the Hilarity Restaurant and a stray cab-tout), toppled heavily out of the portals of that celebrated house of refreshment into the arms of an indulgent policeman.

More life—real life! reflected Daphne, as she laid her head on her pillow, tired out and utterly contented. To-day had yielded its full share. That peculiar but interesting interview with Miss Tallentyre, that glorious carnival under the blue sky at Hurlingham, and that laughter-and-tear-compelling spectacle at the Savoy—all had contributed to the total. Finally, that *tête-à-tête* supper with Jim Carthew—indubitably a dear—ending with the episode of Ally. A little disturbing, that last! Well, perhaps Ally was only trying to see life too, in his own way. Life! Daphne tingled as she felt her own leap in her veins. And to-morrow would bring more!

Then the sandman paid his visit, and she slept like the tired child that she was, having completed to her entire satisfaction another day of what, when you come to think of it, was nothing more or less than an utterly idle, selfish, unprofitable existence.

CHAPTER ELEVEN.

DIES IRAE.

At Belton, Daphne, like her Scriptural counterpart, came to herself. Attired in what she called "rags," she ran wild about the woods and plantations, accompanied by the faithful Mr Dawks, who found a green countryside (even when marred at intervals by a grimy pithead) infinitely preferable to Piccadilly, where the pavement is hot and steerage-way precarious.

They were to stay at Belton till Christmas, after which the house in Berkeley Square would be ready for her. Hitherto she had been well content with the little establishment in Grosvenor Street; but her ideas in certain directions, as her husband had observed to Mrs Carfrae, were developing in a very gratifying manner.

One hot morning Daphne arrived at breakfast half-an-hour late. To do her justice, this was an unusual fault; for in the country she would never have dreamed of indulging in such an urban luxury as breakfast in bed. Her unpunctuality was not due to sloth. She had already superintended the morning toilet of Master Brian Vereker Carr, and had even taken a constitutional with Mr Dawks along the road which ran over the shoulder of a green hill towards Belton Pit, two miles away. She knew that her husband had gone out at seven o'clock to interview the manager at the pithead, and she had reckoned on being picked up by the returning motor and brought home in time for nine o'clock breakfast. Unfortunately Juggernaut had changed his plans and gone to another pit in the opposite direction, with the result that Daphne, besides being compelled to walk twice as far as she intended, found an uncomfortable combination of cold food and chilly husband waiting for her when she reached home.

Juggernaut never called Daphne to book for her shortcomings now. It had become his custom of late, if he found anything amiss in the management of the establishment, to send a message to the housekeeper direct. He should have known better. Daphne, regarding such a proceeding as an imputation of incompetence on her part, boiled inwardly at the slight, though her innate sense of justice told her that it was not altogether undeserved. Being a great success is apt to be a slightly demoralising business, and Daphne herself was beginning dimly to realise the fact. There was no doubt, for instance, that she was not the housekeeper she had been. But what was the good? There had been some credit in feeding the boys and Dad on half nothing, and in conjuring that second weekly joint out of a housekeeping surplus that was a little financial triumph in itself. But now, who cared if a leg of mutton were saved or not? What did it matter if the cook sold the leavings and the butler opened more wine than he decanted? Her husband could afford it. And so on.

A discussion had arisen upon this subject the evening before; and the silent enigmatical man whom she had married, whom she understood so little, and who, from the fact that he treated her as something between an incompetent servant and a spoiled child, appeared to understand her even less, had spoken out more freely than usual, with not altogether happy results. Daphne above all loved openness and candour, and she could not endure to feel that her husband was exercising forbearance towards her, or making allowances, or talking down to her level. Consequently the laborious little lecture she had received, with its studied moderation of tone and its obvious desire to let her down gently, had had an unfortunate but not altogether unnatural result. Juggernaut would have done better to employ his big guns, such as he reserved for refractory public meetings. As it was, Daphne lost her temper.

"Jack," she blazed out suddenly, "I *know* I'm a failure, so why rub it in? I *know* you married me to keep house for you, so you have a perfect right to complain if I do it badly. Well, you have told me; now I know. Shall we drop the subject? I will endeavour to be more competent, honest, and obliging in future."

Juggernaut rose suddenly from the table—they were sitting over their dessert at the time—and walked to the mantelpiece, where he stood leaning his head upon his arms, in an apparent endeavour to mesmerise the fender. Daphne, cooling rapidly, wondered what he was thinking about. Was he angry, or bored, or indifferent?

Presently he turned round.

"I'm afraid I don't handle you as successfully as I handle some other problems, Daphne," he said reflectively. "Good-night!"

That was all. He left the room, and Daphne had not seen him since. Her anger was gone. By bedtime she was thoroughly ashamed of herself, and, being Daphne, no other course lay open to her than that of saying so. Hence her early rising next morning, and her effort to intercept the motor.

The failure of the latter enterprise made matters more difficult; for courage once screwed to the sticking-point and timed for a certain moment cannot as a rule outlast postponement.

Still, she walked into the breakfast-room bravely.

"Jack," she began, a little breathlessly, "I'm sorry I was cross last night."

Her husband was sitting with his back to the door. Possibly if he had seen her face—flushed and appealing under its soft hat of grey *suède*—he might have acted a little more helpfully than he did. He merely laid down his newspaper and remarked cheerfully—

"That is all right, dear. Let us say no more about it. Sit down to your breakfast before it gets colder. You must have been for a long walk. Fried sole or a sausage?"

He rose and helped her to food from the sideboard, as promptly and carefully as if she had been a newly arrived and important guest. It was something; but compared with what he might have done it was nothing. In effect, Daphne had asked for a kiss and had been given a sausage.

It was rather a miserable breakfast. Daphne had vowed to herself not to be angry again: consequently she could only mope. Juggernaut continued to read the newspaper. The political world was in a ferment at the moment. There was a promise for him in all this of work—trouble—the facing of difficulties—the overcoming of strenuous opposition—the joy of battle, in fact. Manlike, he overlooked the trouble that was brewing at his own fireside.

Presently he put down his newspaper and strolled to the open window.

"What a gorgeous day, Daphne. And I have to spend it in a committee-room at Kilchester!"

"Anything important?" asked Daphne, determined to be interested.

"Important? I should just think it was, only people refuse to realise the fact. It's a meeting of the County Territorial Association. What humbug the whole business is! They started the old Volunteers, coddled them, asked nothing of them but a few drills and an annual picnic in camp, and then laughed them out of existence for Saturday-afternoon soldiers. Now they start the Territorials and go to the other extreme. They require of a man that he shall attain, free gratis and for nothing, at the sacrifice of the few scanty weeks which he gets by way of holiday, to practically the same standard of efficiency as a regular soldier, who is paid for it and gets the whole year to do it in. And then they blame us, the County Associations, because we can't find recruits for them! Luckily, we shall have compulsory service soon, and that will end the farce once and for all."

Daphne liked to be talked to like this. In the first place, it removed the uncomfortable and humiliating sensation that she was a child in her husband's eyes; and in the second, it adjusted her sense of proportion as regards the male sex. Obviously, with all these dull but weighty matters to occupy him, a man could not be expected to set such store by conjugal unity as his wife, who had little else to think of.

"Perhaps I have been a little fool," she philosophised. "After all, a man doesn't in the least realise how a woman——"

"What are you going to do to-day?" asked her husband.

"This afternoon I am going over to Croxley Dene to play tennis."

"Anything this morning?"

"I am going to order the motor for twelve o'clock"—rather reluctantly. "I suppose Vick will be back from Kilchester."

"Oh, yes. Are you going out to lunch somewhere?"

"N-no."

"Just a drive?"

"Yes. The fact is," said poor Daphne, hating herself for feeling like a child detected in a fault, "I am going to try my hand at driving the motor myself."

There was a pause, and Juggernaut continued to gaze out of the window, while Daphne pleated the table-cloth.

Presently the hateful expected words came.

"I would rather you didn't."

Daphne rose suddenly to her feet. Her face was aflame, and all her good resolutions had vanished. She had always longed to drive the big car, her appetite having been whetted by occasional experiments upon the property—usually small, easily handled vehicles—of long-suffering friends. She had broached the subject more than once, but had found her husband curiously vague as regards permission. Usually it was "yes" or "no" with him. This morning, tired of the humiliation of constantly asking for leave, she had decided to give orders on her own account. And but for Juggernaut's unlucky question she would have achieved her purpose and settled accounts afterwards—a very different thing from asking leave first, as every child knows.

"And why?" she asked, with suspicious calmness.

"Well, for one thing, I don't think a lady should be seen driving a great covered-in limousine car. You wouldn't go out on the box seat of a brougham, would you? As a matter of fact, if you will have patience for a week or two——"

"Yes, I know!" broke in Daphne passionately. "If I have patience for a week or two, and am a good little girl, and order the meals punctually in the meanwhile, you will perhaps take me for a run one afternoon, and let me hold the wheel while you sit beside me with the second speed in. Thank you! *Good* morning!"

She pushed back her chair, whirled round with a vehement swirl of her tweed skirt, and left the room.

Juggernaut continued to finger a typewritten letter which he had just taken from his pocket. It bore the address of a firm of motor-makers, and said—

"SIR,—We beg to inform you that one of our Handy Runabout 10-12h-p. cars, for which we recently received your esteemed order, is now to hand from the varnishers', and will be delivered at Belton Hall on Tuesday next. As requested, we have given the clutch-pedal and brake a particularly easy spring, with a view to the car being driven by a lady.

"Thanking you for past favours, we are, sir yours faithfully,"

"THE DIABLEMENT-ODORANT
MOTOR CO., LTD."

Juggernaut put the letter back into his pocket.

II.

In due course the Belton motor conveyed its owner to Kilchester and left him there.

"Shall I come back for you, sir?" inquired Mr Vick, the chauffeur. He was a kindly man, despite his exalted station.

"No, thanks—I'll take the train. But I believe Lady Carr wants you to take her over to Croxley Dene this afternoon."

"Her ladyship shall be took," said Mr Vick, with an indulgent smile—Lady Carr was a favourite of his—and forthwith returned to Belton.

On running the car into the yard he found the coachman, Mr Windebank, a sadly diminished luminary in these days, putting a polish upon an unappreciative quadruped.

"You and your machine, Mr Vick," announced Mr Windebank, "is wanted round at twelve sharp."

It was then eleven-fifteen.

"Ho!" replied the ruffled Mr Vick, feeling much as the Emperor Nero might have felt on being requested by the most recently immured early

Christian to see that the arena lions were kept a bit quieter to-morrow night—"ho, indeed!"

"Them's your orders, Mr Vick," said Mr Windebank, resuming the peculiar dental *obligato* which seems to be the inseparable accompaniment of the toilet of a horse, temporarily suspended on this occasion to enable the performer to discharge his little broadside.

Mr Vick turned off various taps and switches on his dash-board, and the humming of the engine ceased.

"I take my orders," he proclaimed in majestic tones, "from the master and missus direct, and from nobody else."

Mr Windebank, after spending some moments in groping for a crushing rejoinder, replied—

"Well, you'd better go inside and get 'em. And you'd better 'ang a nosebag on your sparking-plug in the meanwhile," he added, with sudden and savage irrelevance.

Mr Vick adopted the former of these two suggestions, with the result that at the hour of noon the car slid submissively round to the front of the Hall. Presently Daphne appeared, and disregarding the door which Mr Vick was holding open for her, stepped up into the driver's seat—the throne itself—and took the wheel in her vigorous little hands.

"I am going to drive, Vick," she observed cheerfully.

Mr Vick preserved his self-control and smiled faintly.

"I suppose you have a licence, my lady?" he inquired.

"Gracious, no! I am only just beginning," replied Daphne, who regarded a driver's licence as a sort of reward of merit. "I want you to teach me. Which of these things is the clutch-pedal?"

"The left, my lady. I am afraid," added Mr Vick, with the air of one who intends to stop this nonsense once and for all, "that you will find it very stiff."

"Thanks," said Daphne blandly. "And I suppose the other one is the brake."

"Yes, my lady; but——"

"Then we can start. How do I put in the first speed?"

Mr Vick, in what can only be described as a *moriturus-te-saluto!* voice, gave the required information; and the car, after a dislocating jerk, moved off at a stately four miles per hour. Presently, with much slipping of the clutch and buzzing of the gear-wheels, the second, and finally the third speed went in, and the car proceeded with all the exuberance of its forty-five horse-power down the long straight drive. Fortunately the lodge gates stood open, and the road outside was clear.

Certainly Mr Vick behaved very well. Although every wrench and jar to which his beloved engines were submitted appeared to react directly upon his own internal mechanism, he never winced. Occasionally a muffled groan or a muttered exclamation of "My tyres!" or "My differential!" burst from his overwrought lips; but for the most part he sat like a graven image, merely hoping that when the crash came it would be a good one— something about which it would be really grateful and comforting to say "I told you so!" He also cherished a strong hope that his name would appear in the newspapers.

But Daphne drove well. She had a good head and quick hands; and steering a middle course between the extreme caution of the beginner and the omniscient recklessness of the half-educated, she gave Mr Vick very little excuse for anything in the shape of a genuine shudder. She experienced a little difficulty in getting the clutch right out of action in changing gear; and once she stopped her engine through going round a corner with the brakes on—but that was all. Mr Vick began to feel distinctly aggrieved.

There was a spice of *abandon* in Daphne's present attitude. She had burned her boats; she had flown in the face of authority; and she intended to brazen it out. The breeze whistled in her ears; her eyes blazed; her cheeks glowed. She felt in good fighting trim.

Presently, fetching a compass, the car began to head towards Belton again, and having been directed in masterly fashion through the narrow gates by the back lodge, sped along the final stretch which led to home and luncheon, at a comfortable thirty miles an hour.

At the end of the dappled vista formed by the overarching trees of the avenue appeared a black object, which presently resolved itself into Mr Dawks, lolling comfortably in a patch of sunlight pending his mistress's return.

"Mind the dog, my lady!" cried Mr Vick suddenly.

Daphne had every intention of minding the dog; but desire and performance do not always coincide. Suddenly realizing that Mr Dawks, who was now sitting up expectantly in the middle distance, wagging his tail and extending a welcome as misplaced as that of Jephtha's daughter under somewhat similar circumstances, had no conception of the necessity for vacating his present position, Daphne put down both feet hard and endeavored to bring the car to a standstill. But thirty miles an hour is forty-four feet a second, and the momentum of a car weighing two tons is not lightly to be arrested by a brake constructed only to obey the pressure of a masculine boot. Next moment there was a pathetic little yelp. Daphne had a brief vision of an incredulous and reproachful doggy countenance; the car gave a slight lurch, and then came to full stop, as Mr Vick, having already snapped off the ignition switch on the dashboard, reached across behind Daphne's back and jammed on the side brake.

III.

It was Mr Dawks who really showed to the greatest advantage during the next half-hour. He assured his mistress by every means in his power that the whole thing was entirely his fault; and, like the courteous gentleman that he was, he begged her with faintly wagging tail and affectionate eyes not to distress herself unduly on his account. The thing was done; let there be no more talk about it. It was nothing! By way of showing that the cordiality of their relations was still unimpaired he endeavored to shake hands, first with one paw and then the other; but finding that both were broken he reluctantly desisted from his efforts.

They carried him—what was left of him—into the house, where Daphne, white-faced and tearless, hung in an agony of self-reproach over the friend of her youth—the last link with her girlhood. Dawks lay very still. Once, opening his eyes and evidently feeling that something was expected of him, he licked her hand. The tears came fast after that.

Presently Windebank arrived. He loved all dumb beasts, and was skilled in ministering to their ailments—wherein he transcended that highly educated automaton Mr Vick, to whom the acme of life was represented by a set of perfectly timed sparking-plugs—and he made poor mangled Dawks as comfortable as possible.

"Is he badly hurt, Windebank?" whispered Daphne.

"Yes, miss," said Windebank, touching his forelock. He was a man of few words in the presence of his superiors.

"Will he die?"

Windebank gazed down in an embarrassed fashion at the close coils of fair hair, bowed over the dog's rough coat. Then he stiffened himself defiantly.

"He'll get well right enough, miss," he said with great assurance. "Just wants taking care of, that's all."

It was a lie, and he knew it. But it was a kind lie. To such much is forgiven.

Daphne sat with her patient until three o'clock, and then, overcome with the restlessness of impotent anxiety, and stimulated by an urgent telephonic reminder, ordered out the horses—not the motor.

"Good-bye, old man," she said to Dawks, caressing the dog's long ears and unbecoming nose. "I'll be back in an hour or two. Lie quiet, and you'll soon be all right. Windebank says so."

Mr Dawks whined gently and flapped his tail upon the floor, further intimating by a faint tremor of his ungainly body that if circumstances had permitted he would certainly have made a point of rising and accompanying his mistress to the door and seeing her off the premises. As things were, he must beg to be excused.

Daphne drove to Croxley Dene, where for an hour or so she exchanged banalities with the rest of the county and played a set of tennis.

She drove home in the cool of the evening, more composed in mind. The fresh air and exercise had done her good. Windebank had said that the dog would live: that was everything. Less satisfactory to contemplate was the approaching interview with her husband in the matter of the car. Until now she had not thought of it.

On reaching home she hurried to the library, where she had left the invalid lying on a rug before the fire. Mr Dawks was not there.

"I wonder if Windebank has taken him to the stable," she said to herself. "I'll go and——"

She turned, and found herself face to face with her husband.

"Jack," she asked nervously, "do you know where Dawks is? I suppose you have heard——"

"Yes, I have heard."

Daphne shrank back at the sound of his voice. His face was like flint.

"Then—where is he?" she faltered. "Windebank said——"

"I had him shot."

Daphne stared at him incredulously.

"You had him *shot*?" she said slowly. "*My* Dawks?"

"Yes. It was rank cruelty on your part keeping the poor brute alive, after—after reducing him to that state."

The last half of the sentence may have been natural and justifiable, but no one could call it generous. It is not easy to be merciful when one is at white heat.

Daphne stood up, very slim and straight, gazing stonily into her husband's face.

"Have you buried him?"

"I told one of the gardeners to do so."

"Where?"

"I did not say, but we can———"

"I suppose you know," said Daphne with great deliberation, "that he was the only living creature in all this great house that loved me—really *loved* me?"

Verily, here was war. There was a tense silence for a moment, and an almost imperceptible flicker of some emotion passed over Juggernaut's face. Then he said, with equal deliberation—

"Without any exception?"

"Yes, without *any* exception!" cried poor Daphne, stabbing passionately in the dark. "And since he is dead," she added—"since you have killed him—I am going home to Dad and the boys! They love me!"

She stood before her husband with her head thrown back defiantly, white and trembling with passion.

"Very good. Perhaps that would be best," said Juggernaut quietly.

CHAPTER TWELVE.

CILLY; OR THE WORLD WELL LOST.

"Stiffy," bellowed the new curate ferociously, "what the—I mean, why on earth can't you keep that right foot steady? You edge off to leg every time. If you get a straight ball, stand up to it! If you get a leg-ball, turn round and have a slap at it! But for Heaven's sake don't go running *away*! Especially from things like pats of butter!"

"Awfully sorry, Mr Blunt!" gasped Stiffy abjectly, as another pat of butter sang past his ear. "It's the rotten way I've been brought up! I've never had any decent coaching before. Ough!... No, it didn't hurt a bit, really! I shall be all right in a minute." He hopped round in a constricted circle, apologetically caressing his stomach.

They were in the paddock behind the Rectory orchard. The Reverend Godfrey Blunt, a ruddy young man of cheerful countenance and ingenuous disposition, had rolled out an extremely fiery wicket; and within the encompassing net—Daphne's last birthday present—Stephen Blasius Vereker, impaled frog-wise upon the handle of his bat, and divided between a blind instinct of self-preservation and a desire not to appear ungrateful for favours received, was frantically endeavouring to dodge the deliveries of the church militant as they bumped past his head and ricochetted off his ribs.

"That's better," said Mr Blunt, as his pupil succeeded for the first time in arresting the course of a fast long-hop with his bat instead of his person. "But don't play back to yorkers."

"All right!" said Stiffy dutifully. "I didn't know," he added in all sincerity, "that it was a yorker, or I wouldn't have done it. Oh, I say, well bowled! I don't think anybody could have stopped that one. It never touched the ground at all!"

Stiffy turned round and surveyed his prostrate wickets admiringly. He was an encouraging person to bowl to.

"No, it was a pretty hot one," admitted the curate modestly. "I think I shall have to be going now," he added, mopping his brow. "Parish work, and a sermon to write, worse luck! I think I have just time for a short knock, though. Bowl away, Stiffy!"

He took his stand at the wicket, and after three blind and characteristic swipes succeeded in lifting a half-volley of Stiffy's into the adjacent orchard. When the bowler, deeply gratified with a performance of which he felt himself to be an unworthy but necessary adjunct, returned ten minutes later from a successful search for the ball, he found his hero hastily donning the old tweed jacket and speckled straw hat which he kept for wear with his cricket flannels.

"Hallo! Off?" cried Stiffy regretfully.

"Yes; I'm afraid so," replied Mr Blunt. He was gazing anxiously through a gap in the hedge which commanded the Rectory garden-gate. "This is my busy day. So long, old man!"

He vaulted the fence, and set off down the road at a vigorous and businesslike trot. But after a hundred yards or so he halted, and looked round him with an air which can only be described as furtive. Before him the road, white and dusty, continued officiously on its way to the village and duty. Along the right-hand side thereof ran a neat rail-fence, skirting the confines of Tinkler's Den. The landscape appeared deserted. All nature drowsed in the hot afternoon sun.

Mr Blunt, who was a muscular young Christian, took a running jump of some four feet six, cleared the topmost rail, and landed neatly on the grassy slope which ran down towards the Den.

"Now then, Sunny Jim!" remarked a reproving voice above his head, "*pas si beaucoup de cela!*"

However sound our nervous systems may be, we are all of us liable to be startled at times. Mr Blunt was undoubtedly startled on the occasion, and being young and only very recently ordained, signified the same in the usual manner.

When he looked up into the tree where Nicky was reclining, that virtuous damsel's fingers were in her ears.

"Mr Blunt," she remarked, "I am both surprised and shocked."

"Veronica Vereker," replied Mr Blunt, turning and shaking his fist as he retreated down the slope towards Tinkler's Den, "next time I get hold of you I will wring your little neck!"

Miss Veronica Vereker kissed the tips of her fingers to him.

"We will now join," she proclaimed, in a voice surprisingly reminiscent of the throaty tenor which Mr Blunt reserved for his ecclesiastical performances, "in singing Hymn number two hundred and thirty-three;

during which those who desire to leave the church are recommended to do so, as it is *my—turn—to—preach—the—sermon*!"

But by this time the foe, running rapidly, was out of earshot.

Half-an-hour later Stiffy, who was a gregarious animal, went in search of his younger sister, whom he discovered, recently returned from her sylvan skirmish with the curate, laboriously climbing into a hammock in the orchard.

"Nicky, will you come and play cricket?" he asked politely.

"I suppose that means will I come and bowl to you?" replied Nicky.

"No. You can bat if you like."

"Well, I won't do either," said Nicky agreeably.

"What shall we do, then?" pursued Stiffy, with unimpaired *bonhomie*.

"Personally, I am going to remain in this hammock," replied the lady. "I recommend you, dear, to go and put your head in a bucket. *Good* afternoon! Sorry you can't stop."

"I wonder if Cilly would play," mused Stiffy.

"Cilly? I don't think! She is gloating over her clothes in her bedroom. If you and I, my lad," continued Veronica reflectively, "were going to be presented at Court next week, I wonder if we should make such unholy shows of ourselves for days beforehand."

"I know her boxes are all packed," pursued Stiffy hopefully, "because I went and sat on the lids myself after lunch. Perhaps she will come out for half-an-hour before tea. Dad and Tony won't be back from Tilney till seven, so they are no good."

"Well, run along, little man," said Nicky, closing her eyes. "I'm fed up with you."

Stiffy departed obediently, and for ten minutes his younger sister reclined in her hammock, her sinful little soul purged for the moment of evil intent against any man. When next she opened her eyes Stiffy was standing disconsolately before her.

"Go away," said Nicky faintly. "We have no empty bottles or rabbit-skins at present. If you call round about Monday we shall be emptying the dustbin——"

"Cilly's not there," said Stiffy. "Keziah thinks she has gone out for a walk. She saw her strolling down towards the Den half-an-hour ago."

"*The Den?*" Nicky's eyes suddenly unclosed to their full radius. "My che-ild! So *that's* the game! *That* was why the pale young curate was jumping fences. Ha, *ha*! Stiffy, would you like some fun?"

Stiffy, mystified but docile, assented.

"We are going," announced Nicky, rolling gracefully out of the hammock, "to stalk a brace of true lovers."

"What—Mr Blunt and Cilly? Do you mean——? Are they really keen on each other?" inquired the unobservant male amazedly.

"*Are* they? My lad, it has been written all over them for weeks! I'm not certain, though," continued the experienced Nicky, "that the poor dears are aware of it themselves yet. But to-day is Cilly's last for months, so——"

"Do you mean they are down in the Den together?" demanded Stiffy.

"I do."

"But—Mr Blunt has gone off to do parish work. He told me so himself."

"Parish work my foot!" commented Nicky simply. "Come on! Let's go and mark down their trail! We can pretend to be Red Indians, if you like," she added speciously.

But the sportsmanlike Stiffy hung back.

"Let's play cricket instead," he said hesitatingly.

"Not me! Come on!"

"Nicky," said Stiffy, searching his hand, so to speak, for trumps, "Preston is killing a pig this afternoon at four o'clock. I've just remembered. He promised not to begin till I came. We shall just be in time. Hurry up!"

"I am going," said Nicky firmly, "to stalk that couple. Are you coming?"

"No. It's not playing the game," said Stiffy bravely.

Nicky, uneasily conscious that he spoke the truth, smiled witheringly.

"All right, milksop!" she said. "I shall go by myself. You can go and hold the pig's hand."

So they departed on their several errands.

Meanwhile Cilly and the curate sat side by side beneath a gnarled and venerable oak in Tinkler's Den.

..."Then your name is called out," continued Cilly raptly, "and you give one last squiggle to your train and go forward and curtsey—to *all* the Royalties in turn, I think, but I'm not quite sure about that part yet—and then you pass along out of the way, and somebody picks up your train and throws it over your shoulder, and you find yourself in another room, and it's all over. Won't it be heavenly?"

"Splendid!" replied Mr Blunt, without enthusiasm.

"After that," continued Cilly, "my sister is going to take me simply everywhere. And I am to meet lots of nice people. It's too late for Henley and Ascot and that sort of thing this summer, but I am to have them all next year. Later on, we are going to Scotland. I'm not at all a lucky girl, am I?"

It was one of those questions to which, despite its form, an experienced Latin grammarian would have unhesitatingly prefixed the particle *nonne*. But the Reverend Godfrey Blunt merely replied in a hollow voice—

"What price me?"

Cilly, startled, turned and regarded his hot but honest face, and then lowered her gaze hastily to the region of her own toes.

The Reverend Godfrey was a fine upstanding young man, with merry grey eyes; and there was a cheerful and boisterous *bonhomie* about his conversation which the exigencies of his calling had not yet intoned out of him. No one had ever considered him brilliant, for his strength lay in character rather than intellect. He was a perfect specimen of that unromantic but priceless type with which our public schools and universities never fail to meet the insatiable demands of a voracious Empire. The assistant-commissioner, the company officer, the junior form-master, the slum-curate—these are they that propel the ship of State. Up above upon the quarter-deck, looking portentously wise and occasionally quarrelling for the possession of the helm, you may behold their superiors—the Cabinet Minister, the Prelate, the Generalissimo. But our friends remain below the water-line, unheeded, uncredited, and see to it that the wheels go round. They expect no thanks, and they are not disappointed. The ship goes forward, and that is all they care about. Of such is the British Empire.

The Reverend Godfrey Blunt was one of this nameless host. At school he had scraped into the Sixth by a hair's-breadth; at the University he had secured a degree of purely nominal value. He had been an unheroic member of his House eleven; thereafter he had excoriated his person uncomplainingly and unsuccessfully upon a fixed seat for the space of three years, not because he expected to make bumps or obtain his Blue, but because his College second crew had need of him. Since then he had worked for five years in a parish in Bermondsey, at a stipend of one hundred pounds a-year; and only the doctor's ultimatum had prevailed on him to try country work for a change. His spelling was shaky, his theology would have made Pusey turn in his grave, and his sermons would have bored his own mother. But he was a man.

Cilly, whom we left bashfully contemplating her shoe-buckles under an oak-tree, was conscious of a new, sudden, and disturbing thrill. Young girls are said seldom to reflect and never to reason. They have no need. They have methods of their own of arriving at the root of the matter. Cilly realised in a flash that if a proper man was the object of her proposed journey through the great and enticing world before her, she need never set out at all. Something answering to that description was sitting beside her, sighing like a furnace. Her face flamed.

"What did you say?" she inquired unsteadily.

"I said 'What price me?'" reiterated the curate mournfully.

"What do you mean?"

"I mean——" he spoke hesitatingly, like a man picking his words from an overwhelming crowd of applicants—"well, I mean this. You and I have seen a lot of each other since I came here. You have been awfully good to me, and I have got into the way of bringing you my little troubles, and turning to you generally if I felt dismal or humpy. (There *are* more joyful spots, you know, to spend one's leisure hours in than Mrs Tice's first-floor-front.) And now—now you are going away from me, to meet all sorts of attractive people and have the time of your life. You will have a fearful lot of attention paid to you. Nine out of ten men you meet will fall in love with you——"

"Oh! nonsense!" said Cilly feebly.

"But I *know* it," persisted Blunt. "I simply can't conceive any man being able to do anything else. Do you know——" the words stuck in his throat for a moment and then came with a rush—"do you know that you are the most adorable girl on God's earth? I love you! I love you! *There*—I've said it! I had meant to say a lot more first—work up to it by degrees, you know—but it has carried me away of its own accord. I love you—dear, *dear* Cilly!"

There was a long stillness. All nature seemed to be watching with bated breath for the next step. Only above their heads the branches of the oak-tree crackled gently. Cilly's head swam. Something new and tremulous was stirring within her. She closed her eyes, lest the spell should be broken by the sight of some mundane external object. A purely hypothetical fairy prince, composed of equal parts of Peer of the Realm, Lifeguardsman, Mr Sandow, Lord Byron, and the Bishop of London, whom she had cherished in the inmost sanctuary of her heart ever since she had reached the age at which a girl begins to dream about young men, suddenly rocked upon his pedestal. Then she opened her eyes again, and contemplated the homely features of the Reverend Godfrey Blunt.

Not that they appeared homely any longer. Never had a man's face undergone such a transformation in so short a time. To her shy eyes he had grown positively handsome. Cilly felt her whole being suddenly drawn towards this goodly youth. The composite paragon enshrined in her heart gave a final lurch and then fell headlong, to lie dismembered and disregarded, Dagon-like, at the foot of his own pedestal.

...Slowly their hands met, and they gazed upon one another long and rapturously. How long, they did not know. There was no need to take count of time. They seemed to be sitting together all alone on the edge of the universe, with eternity before them. The next step was obvious enough; they both realised what it must be: but they did not hurry. They sat on, this happy pair, waiting for inspiration.

It came—straight from above their heads.

"Kiss her, you fool!" commanded a hoarse and frenzied voice far up the tree.

Crackle! Crash! *Bump!*

And Nicky, overestimating in her enthusiasm the supporting power of an outlying branch, tumbled, headlong but undamaged, a medley of arms and legs and blue pinafore, right at their feet.

A few hours later Daphne, preceded by a rather incoherent telegram, drove up to the Rectory in the station fly.

She was met at the door by Cilly, and the two, as if by one impulse, fell into each other's arms.

"Daphne, *dear* Daph," murmured the impetuous Cilly, "I am the happiest girl in all the world."

"And I," said Daphne simply, "am the most miserable."

CHAPTER THIRTEEN.

THE COUNTERSTROKE.

The scene is the Restaurant International, a palatial house of refreshment in Regent Street; the time half-past one. At a table in the corner of the Grand Salle à Manger, set in a position calculated to extract full value from the efforts of a powerful orchestra, a waiter of majestic mien, with a powdered head, and a gold tassel on his left shoulder, stands towering over two recently arrived patrons with the *menu*.

The patrons, incredible as it may appear, are Stephen Blasius Vereker and Veronica Elizabeth Vereker. Stiffy, in the gala dress of a schoolboy of eighteen, is perspiring freely under the gaze of the overpowering menial at his elbow; Nicky, in a new hat of colossal but correct dimensions (the gift of her eldest sister), with her hair gathered into the usual *ne plus ultra* of the "flapper,"—a constricted pigtail tied with a large black bow of ribbon,—is entirely unruffled.

How they got there will appear presently.

"Will you lunch *à la carte* or *table d'hôte*, sir?" inquired the waiter, much as an executioner might say—"Will you be drawn or quartered?"

The flustered Stiffy gazed helplessly at his sister.

"He means, will you pay for what you eat or eat what you pay for, dear," explained that experienced and resourceful young person. "You must excuse him," she added, turning her round and trustful orbs upon the waiter. "He is not accustomed to being given a choice of dishes."

The waiter, realising that here was a worthy opponent, maintained a countenance of wood and repeated the question.

"You had better give *me* the *menu*," said Miss Vereker. "How much is the *table d'hôte* lunch?"

"Four shillings, madam."

Madam mused.

"Let me see," she said thoughtfully. "Can we run to it, dear?"

"Of course!" said Stiffy in an undertone, reddening with shame. "You know Daphne gave me——"

Nicky smiled joyfully.

"So she did. I had forgotten. Two and nine, wasn't it?"

Stiffy, with a five-pound-note crackling in his pocket, merely gaped.

"Then," continued Nicky, calculating on her fingers, "there is the three and a penny which we got out of the missionary-box. That makes five and tenpence. And there is that shilling that slipped down into your boot, Stiffy. You can easily get under the table and take it off. Six and tenpence. I have elevenpence in stamps, and that, with the threepenny-bit we picked up off the floor of the bus, makes eight shillings. We can just do it. Thank you," she intimated to the waiter with a seraphic smile—"we will take *table d'hôte*. I suppose," she added wistfully, "there would be no reduction if I took my little boy on my knee?"

"None, madam."

And the waiter, still unshaken, departed to bring the *hors d'œuvres*.

"Nicky, don't play the goat!" urged the respectable Stephen in a low and agitated voice. "That blighter really *believes* we are going to pay him in stamps. We shall get flung out, for a cert!"

"It's all right," said Nicky. "I am only going to try and make him laugh."

"You'll fail," said her brother with conviction.

At this moment a mighty tray, covered with such inducements to appetite as anchovies, sliced tomatoes, sardines, radishes, chopped celery, Strasburg sausage, *et hoc genus omne*—all equally superfluous in the case of a schoolboy up in town on an *exeat*—was laid before him with a stately flourish. Then the waiter came stiffly and grimly to attention, and stood obviously expectant. *Hors d'œuvres* are rather puzzling things. Here was a chance for the tyros before him to show their mettle.

They showed it.

"One gets tired of these everlasting things," mused Nicky wearily. "I'll just peck at one or two. You can fetch the soup, waiter: we shall be ready for it immediately."

"Thick or clear soup, madam?"

"We'll have thick to begin with, please: then clear," replied Nicky calmly. "Stiffy, I will take an anchovy."

The waiter was not more than two minutes absent, but ere he returned a lightning transformation scene had been enacted.

Certainly the Briton, with all his faults, surpasses the foreigner in the control of the emotions. What a Gaul or a Teuton would have done on witnessing the sight which met the eyes of the imperturbable Ganymede of the Restaurant International when he returned with the thick soup, it is difficult to say. The first would probably have wept, the second have sent for a policeman. For lo! the richly dight *hors d'œuvres* tray had become a solitude—the component parts thereof were duly discovered by the charwoman next morning amid the foliage of an adjacent palm—and the tail of the last radish was disappearing into Stiffy's mouth. Stiffy, once roused, made an excellent accomplice, though he had no initiative of his own.

The waiter's face twitched ever so slightly, and there was an undulating movement in the region of his scarlet waistcoat. But he recovered himself in time, and having served the thick soup, departed unbidden in search of the clear.

"Nicky," said Stiffy in a concerned voice, "are we really going to have everything on the *menu*?"

"You are, my son," replied Nicky. "I, being a lady, will make use of this palm-tub."

The waiter brought the clear soup, and asked for instructions with regard to the fish.

"What sort of fish have you?"

The man proffered the card.

"*Sole: Sauce Tartare.* That means sole with tartar sauce," Nicky translated glibly for the benefit of her untutored relative. "We had better not have that. Tartar sauce always makes him sick," she explained to the waiter, indicating the fermenting Stiffy. "What else is there? Let me see—ah! *Blanchailles!*—er—*Blanchailles!* A very delicate fish! Quite so. You may bring us"—her brain worked desperately behind a smiling face, but fruitlessly— "a *blanchaille*, waiter."

There was an ominous silence. Then the waiter asked, in a voice tinged with polite incredulity—

"A *whole* one each, madam?"

"Certainly," said madam in freezing tones.

The waiter bowed deferentially, and departed.

"Stiffy," inquired Nicky in agonised tones, "what *is* a *blanchaille*? Don't say it's a cod!"

Stiffy devoted three hours a-week to the study of Modern Languages, but so far no *blanchaille* has swum into his vocabulary.

"I've a notion," he said after a prolonged mental effort, "that it is a sturgeon."

"How big is a sturgeon?"

"It's about the size of a shark, I think."

"Mercy! And we have ordered a whole one each!"

But their capacity was not to be taxed after all. The waiter returned, and with the nonchalant demeanour of a hardened clubman playing out an unexpected ace of trumps, laid down two plates. In the centre of each reposed a single forlorn diminutive whitebait.

But it was here that Veronica Elizabeth Vereker rose to her greatest heights. She inspected her own portion and then her brother's.

"Waiter," she said at last, "will you kindly take away this young gentleman's fish and ask the cook to give you a rather longer one? About three-quarters of an inch, I should say. The child"—indicating her hirsute and crimson senior—"gets very peevish and fretful if his portion is smaller than any one else's."

Without a word the waiter picked up Stiffy's plate and bore it away. His broad back had become slightly bowed, and his finely chiselled legs had a warped and bandy appearance. The strain was telling.

Stiffy gazed upon his sister in rapt admiration.

"Nicky, you *ripper!*" he said.

After this it was mere child's play to request a stout gentleman with a chain round his neck to submit the wine list—an imposing volume of many pages—and after a heated and highly technical discussion on the respective merits of Pommery and Cliquot, to order one stone-ginger and two glasses.

Nicky next instructed the waiter to present her compliments to the leader of the band, and to request as a special favour that he and his colleagues would oblige with a rendering of *Shall We Gather at the River?* The waiter returned with a reply to the effect that the *chef d'orchestre* would be delighted. Unfortunately he had not the full score by him at the moment, but had sent along to the Café Royal to borrow a copy. Everything would be in readiness about tea-time. It was then a little after two, and it was admitted by both Nicky and Stiffy that honours on this occasion were divided.

So far both sides, as the umpires say on Territorial field-days, had acquitted themselves in a manner deserving great credit; but the waiter scored the odd and winning trick a little later, in a particularly subtle manner. Age and experience always tell. Nicky, unduly inflated by early success, insisted upon

Stiffy ordering a liqueur with his coffee. Green Chartreuse was finally selected and brought.

"Shall I pour it into your coffee, sir?" asked the waiter respectfully.

"Please," said the unsuspecting Stiffy.

The man obeyed, and directly afterwards emitted a sound which caused both children to glance up suddenly. They glared suspiciously, first at one another, then at the back of the retreating foe.

"Do people drink Green Chartreuse *in* their coffee?" asked Nicky apprehensively.

"I don't know," said Stiffy. He tasted the compound. "No, I'm *blowed* if they do! Nicky, we've been had. He's one up!"

"It would score him off," replied the undefeated Nicky, "if you could manage to be sick."

But Stiffy held out no hope of this happy retaliation; and they ultimately produced the five-pound note and paid the score with somewhat chastened mien, adding a *douceur* which was as excessive as it was unnecessary. Waiters do not get much entertainment out of serving meals as a rule.

II.

"Now we must meet Daphne," said Stiffy, as they left the restaurant and hailed a cab.

They were in town for an all-too-brief sojourn of twenty-four hours, to assist at the inspection of Daphne's new house. It was now February, and Lady Carr had not seen her husband since the eruption at Belton last summer. Juggernaut had made no attempt to prevent her going home, and when she wrote later, requesting that Master Brian Vereker Carr might be sent to her, had despatched him without remonstrance. No one save Cilly and her beloved Godfrey—least of all the Rector—knew of the true state of affairs; and all during that autumn and winter Daphne was happier in a fashion than she had ever been. To a large extent she resumed command of the household, setting Cilly free for other very right and natural diversions; and a sort of *édition de luxe* of the old days came into being, with first-hand food at every meal and a boy to clean the boots and drive the pony.

Daphne was entirely impervious to the gravity of the situation. There are certain women who are curiously wanting in all sense of responsibility. They preserve the child's lack of perspective and proportion even after they grow up, and the consequences are sometimes disastrous. If love arrives upon the scene no further harm ensues, for the missing qualities spring up, with that Jonah's-gourd-like suddenness which characterises so many feminine developments, at the first touch of the great magician's wand. The retarded faculties achieve maturity in a flash, and their owner becomes maternal, solicitous, Martha-like; and all is well.

Daphne was one of these women; but so far, unfortunately, she had failed to fall in love. Her marriage had never really touched her. Her husband had vibrated many strings in her responsive impulsive young heart—gratitude, affection, admiration,—but the great harmonious combination, the master-chord, had yet to be struck. Consequently she saw nothing unusual in living apart from her husband, financing her family with his money, and enjoying herself with friends whom he did not know.

Early in the year, however, it occurred to her that it would be pleasant to go home again for a time. Her elastic nature had entirely recovered from the stress of last summer's crisis, and she was frankly consumed with curiosity on the subject of the new house in Berkeley Square—and said so. It was perhaps an unfortunate reason for a wife to give for wishing to return to her husband, but this did not occur to her at the time. She received a brief note in reply, saying that the furnishing and decorating were now practically completed, and the house was ready for her inspection any time she cared to come up to town. Hence this joyous expedition.

Daphne had half expected to find her husband waiting for her at the house, for the Parliamentary recess was over and she knew he was almost certain to be in town. Instead, she was received by an overwhelmingly polite individual named Hibbins, from the house-furnishers. Mr Hibbins' appearance and deportment proved a sore trial to the composure of Nicky, who exploded at frequent and unexpected intervals throughout the afternoon, lamely alleging the fantastic design of some very ordinary wallpaper or the shortness of Stiffy's Sunday trousers in excuse.

It was essentially a masculine house, furnished in accordance with the man's ideas of solidity and comfort. The high oak panelling and dark-green frieze in the dining-room pleased Daphne, who recognised that glass and silver, well-illuminated, would show up bravely in such a setting. The drawing-room was perhaps a little too severe in its scheme of decoration: Daphne would have preferred something more feminine. "But that comes," she reflected characteristically, "of leaving the declaration to your partner!" There was a billiard-room in which Nicky declared it would be a sin to place a billiard-table, so perfectly was it adapted for waltzing after dinner.

Opening out of the billiard-room was a plainly furnished but attractive little set of apartments—"the bachelor suite" Mr Hibbins designated it—consisting of a snug study with an apartment adjoining, containing a small camp-bed and a large bath. Daphne's own rooms consisted of a bedroom and boudoir on the first floor, with wide bow-windows.

The nursery came last. It was a large irregular-shaped room at the top of the house, full of unexpected corners and curious alcoves such as children love, affording convenient caves for robbers and eligible lairs for wild beasts, fabulous or authentic. In addition to the regulation nursery furniture there was a miniature set, in green-stained wood—a table barely eighteen inches high, a tiny arm-chair, and a pigmy sofa upon which Master Brian's friends might recline when they came to drink tea, or its equivalent. Round the whole room ran a brightly coloured dado covered with life-size figures of all the people we love when we are young—Jack the Giant-Killer, Old King Cole, Cinderella, and the Three Bears. Even Peter Pan, with residence and following, was there. The spectacle of Doctor Johnson taking a walk down Fleet Street would pale to insignificance compared with that of Master Brian Vereker Carr enjoying a constitutional along his own dado, encountering a new friend round every corner.

Daphne suddenly realised that here was yet another aspect of this strange, impenetrable husband of hers. The room in its way was a work of genius— the genius that understands children.

As they departed to catch the afternoon train to Snayling the obsequious Mr Hibbins produced a letter.

Sir John Carr, he explained, had called at the head office of their firm that morning—in *person*, Mr Hibbins added with a gratified smile—and requested that this letter should be handed to her ladyship in the afternoon. Sir John had also instructed Mr Hibbins to inform her ladyship that any improvements or alterations which she desired had only to be mentioned to be carried out.

Mr Hibbins having handed them into a cab and bidden them an unctuous farewell, they drove away to the station, Nicky atoning for previous aloofness by hanging out of the window and waving her handkerchief until they turned the corner.

III.

The journey from London to Snayling, involving as it does a run of forty miles by main line, a wait of indefinite duration at a junction furnished with no other facilities for recreation than a weighing-machine and a printed and detailed record of the fate which awaits persons who compass the awe-inspiring but cumbrous crime of travelling-by-a-class-superior-to-that-to-which-the-ticket-in-their-possession-entitles-them, and concluding with an interminable crawl along a branch line, is not at first sight an enterprise that promises much joyous adventure; but Nicky and Stiffy, who usually contrived to keep *ennui* at arm's-length, had a very tolerable time of it.

Their efforts at first were directed to securing an apartment to themselves—an achievement which, when you come to think of it, fairly epitomises the Englishman's outlook on life in general.

"Hang your face out of the window, Stiffy, my lad," commanded Nicky, returning from an unsuccessful attempt to wheedle the guard into labelling their carriage "engaged," "and play at Horatius Cocles till the train starts. That ought to do the trick."

But no. At the last moment a crusty-looking old gentleman wrenched the door open, nearly precipitating Horatius Cocles (and face) on to the platform, and sat down with great determination in the corner seat. He glared ferociously at the demure-looking pair before him, in a manner which intimated plainly that he was too old a customer to be kept out of his usual compartment by tricks of *that* kind. After this he produced *The Westminster Gazette* from a handbag and began to read it.

Nicky gave him five minutes. Then, turning to her brother and scrutinising his freckled countenance, she observed in clear and measured tones—

"I think they have let you out rather *soon*, John."

Stiffy, realising that he was the person addressed and that some fresh game was afoot, looked as intelligent as possible, and waited. Daphne, in the far corner of the carriage, hurriedly opened her husband's letter and began to read it.

"The marks aren't all gone yet," continued Nicky, inspecting her brother anxiously. "Are you still peeling?"

"Yes—I think so," said Stiffy, groping for his cue.

"Ah!" Nicky nodded her head judicially. "We must give you a carbolic bath when we get you home."

The Westminster Gazette emitted a perceptible crackle.

"It will never do," pursued Nicky, getting into her stride, "to have you disfigured for life."

Stiffy, who was impervious to all reflections upon his personal appearance, grinned faintly. Opposite, a scared and bulging eye slid cautiously round the edge of *The Westminster Gazette*, and embarked upon a minute and apprehensive inspection of the plague-stricken youth. Nicky saw, and thrilled with gratification. She was on the point of continuing when the train dived into a tunnel. Having no desire that her schemes should go awry in the din, she waited.

The train came to a sudden and unexplained stop. Deathlike silence reigned, broken only by murmurs of conversation from next door. Presently in the gross darkness Nicky's voice was once more uplifted.

"By the way, is it infectious, or merely *contagious*? I meant to ask when I called for you at the Institute"—she was rather proud of that inspiration: an Institute sounded more terrifying and mysterious than a Hospital—"but in the excitement of that last fainting-fit of yours I forgot. Which is it?"

"Both, I think," said Stiffy, anxious to help.

"Ah! I feared as much. Still, things might be worse," commented Nicky philosophically. "So many of these complaints are infectious in the early stages, when no one suspects any trouble. Mumps, for instance, or scarlet fever. But others, like yours, are only dangerous in the convalescent stage, and then of course one knows exactly where one is."

There was a crumpling of paper in the darkness, accompanied by a shuffling of feet and a vibratory motion of the seat-cushions—all indicative of the presence of one who knows exactly where *he* is, and regrets the fact exceedingly.

"The air is very close in here," resumed Nicky's voice. "I wonder——" she whispered a sentence into Stiffy's ear, the only distinguishable word in which was "germs." "Of course, I have *had* it—slightly," she added in a relieved tone.

Something moved again in the darkness opposite to them, and then came a sound as of a window being cautiously slid open.

"Still, I *think*," replied Stiffy solicitously—as usual he was warming up to the game slowly but surely—"that it would be wiser for you to keep your mouth closed and breathe through your nose. One cannot be too careful."

"All right," said Nicky.

Once again silence reigned. But presently there fell upon the ears of the conspirators, rendered almost incredulous by joy, an unmistakable and stertorous sound, as of some heavy and asthmatic body taking in air through unaccustomed channels.

Five minutes later the train, groaning arthritically, resumed its way and crawled out of the tunnel into a station. Nicky and Stiffy, blinking in the sudden daylight, beheld the reward of their labours. A corpulent and rapidly ageing citizen, shrinking apprehensively into a corner of the compartment and holding a small handbag upon his knees as if with a view to instant departure, sat glaring malignantly upon them. His face was mottled, his mouth was firmly closed, and he breathed perseveringly through his nostrils.

Next moment he had flung open the door and was out upon the platform, inhaling great gulps of vernal air and looking for the station-master.

"Stiffy, you darling! I'll never call you a fat-head again!" declared Nicky, enthusiastically embracing her complacent accomplice. "That notion of yours was simply *It!* Daph, wasn't it splen—Hallo! Bless me, Stiffy, if Daph isn't breathing through her nose too! Look!"

Certainly Daphne's lips were tightly compressed, but she turned to her companions and smiled faintly.

"It's all right, kids," she said; "I think this carriage is overheated or something. I shall be all right in a minute. Keep that window open, Stiffy dear."

She was very white, but on emphatically declining Nicky's offer of first aid she was left to herself, while her brother and sister discussed the course to be followed in the event of another invasion of the carriage. Like true artists, they scorned to achieve the same effect by the same means twice running.

Meanwhile Daphne re-read her husband's letter.

"... I have waited six months, and as you display no inclination to look facts in the face, I am compelled to take the initiative myself. As far as I can gather from your attitude, you seem to consider that things are very well as they are. On this point I beg to differ from you. The present situation must *end*. We must either come together again or part for good on some definitely arranged terms.

"... As you have exhibited no desire to reconcile yourself to me—your letter indicates that your sole object in returning home is to play with your latest toy, the new house—I conclude that you wish to remain your own mistress. I therefore place the new house entirely at your disposal. You can draw money as you require it from Coutts', and I will see to it that there is always an adequate balance. I think, if you have no objection, that it would be as well if I occasionally came to the house, and occupied the bachelor suite off the billiard-room; but I shall come and go without troubling you. We ought to make this concession to appearances.

"I should not like your father, for instance, to be made unhappy by the knowledge that his daughter and her husband found it better to go their several ways.

"... As for the custody of the boy——"

A long, slow shudder rippled down Daphne's spine. Custody! There was a horrible legal, end-of-all-things, divorce-court flavour about the word.

"I think it would be a good scheme, Stiffy dear," broke in Nicky's cheerful voice, "for you to pretend this time that you have just been discharged from an asylum. I will be taking you home, and ..." Her voice faded.

" ... You will naturally like to have him with you while he is a mere child. I will therefore leave him in your hands for the present. Later, when he goes to a public school and University, I think I should like him to be with me during his holidays. When he grows up altogether, he must please himself about——."

Public School! University! Daphne turned sick and faint. Were the provisions of this merciless letter to cover all eternity? What had she done to deserve this?

"It would be a bright thought," continued Nicky's voice, returning from a great distance, "to roll up your handkerchief into a ball and put it right into your mouth. Then do something to attract their attention, and when they are all looking, pull it right out with a jerk, and mop and mow. *Can* you mop and mow, Stiffy? Mop, anyhow! Just before a station, you know, so that they can get out. If that doesn't work, roll about on the cushions, and——."

Daphne detached her gaze from the flying landscape, and finished the letter.

"Forgive me if I appear to have resorted to extreme or harsh measures. I suppose I am a hard man: at any rate, I am not pliable. I dare say if I had been differently built I might have played the part of the modern husband with fair success, and you could have picked your companions at will. Unfortunately, I would rather die than permit you to impose such a *régime* upon me, as you seem prepared to do. The thing is degrading. To my mind there can be no compromise, no half-measures, between man and wife. It must be all in all, or not at all....

"Lastly, Daphne, let me say how sorry I am that things have come to this pass. I realise that it is my fault. I should not have asked a young and inexperienced girl to marry me. You could not be expected to know better: I might and should. And it is because I realise and admit that the fault is mine, that I refrain from "attaching any blame to you or uttering any reproaches. All I can do is to say that I am sorry, and make it possible for you to go your way, unhampered as far as may be by the ties of a marriage which should never have taken place.

"If I can at any time be of service to you, command me. I can never forget that we have had our happy hours together."

Daphne folded up the letter with mechanical deliberation. The first numbness was over. Her brain was clear again, and thoughts were crowding in upon her. But two things overtopped all the others for the moment.

The first was the realisation of the truth of her husband's words. The old situation *had* been impossible—as impossible as the new one was inevitable. She saw that—at last. "All in all, or not at all," he had said, and he was right.

The second was a sudden awakening to the knowledge that we never begin really to want a thing in this world until we find we cannot have it.

CHAPTER FOURTEEN.

INTERVENTION.

"Madame," announced the major-domo of the Hôtel Magnifique with a superb gesture, "the post from England!"

"Thank you, Thémistocle," said Mrs Carfrae. "But you are over-generous: one of these letters is not for me."

She handed back an envelope.

Thémistocle, needless to remark, was desolated at his own carelessness, and said so. But the old lady cut him short.

"Don't distress yourself unduly, Thémistocle. It is a mistake even an English body might have made. There is not much difference between Carfrae and Carthew."

The punctilious Thémistocle refused to be comforted.

"But no, madame," he persisted; "I should have observed that the letter addressed itself to a monsieur, and not a madame. Doubtless it is intended for one of the English party who arrive this afternoon."

"An English party? Is my seclusion to be disturbed by the disciples of the good Monsieur Cook?"

"Assuredly no, madame. These are English milords from Marseilles. The Riviera season has been a failure: the mistral blows eternally. Therefore the party abandons Cannes and telegraphs for apartments at the Hôtel Magnifique."

"Are they from London? Possibly I may be acquainted with some of them. What are their names?"

Thémistocle would inquire. He departed amid a whirlwind of bows, leaving Mrs Carfrae to continue her *déjeûner* in the sunny verandah of her sitting-room. She came to Algiers every spring, and she came unattended save for a grim-faced Scottish maid of her own age. It was Mrs Carfrae's habit to assume that she and her wheeled chair were a drag upon the world; and she systematically declined invitations to join friends upon the Riviera. People, she explained, who would otherwise have been playing tennis at the Beau Site or roulette at the Casino would feel bound to relinquish these pursuits and entertain her. So she came to Algiers by herself, this proud, lonely old lady.

"Carthew?" she mused. "That is the name of Johnny Carr's familiar spirit. And that letter was in Johnny's handwriting. Well, Thémistocle, who are— stand *still*, man!"

Thémistocle reluctantly curtailed an elaborate obeisance, and came to attention. The leader of the expedition, he announced, was Milord the Right Hon. Sir Hilton Bart., with Milady Hilton Bart. The names of the other guests were not known, but there were eleven of them.

They arrived on the steamer that afternoon, and drove in an imposing procession up the long and dusty hill that leads to Mustapha Supérieur, leaving Algiers—that curious combination of Mauretanian antiquity and second-rate French provincialism—baking peacefully in the hot sunshine below. As Thémistocle had predicted, they came unshepherded by the good Mr Cook. They were of the breed and caste that has always found its own way about the world.

There was Sir Arthur Hilton, a slow-moving Briton of few words, with a pretty wife of complementary volubility. There were one or two soldiers on leave; there was a Cambridge don; there were three grass widows. There were two newly emancipated schoolgirls, gobbling life in indigestible but heavenly lumps. There was a tall and beautiful damosel, with a demeanour which her admirers—and they were many—described as regal, and which her detractors—and their name was legion—described as affected; and whom her chaperon, Lady Hilton, addressed as "Nina, dearest." And there was a squarely built, freckle-faced young man with whom we are already acquainted. His name was Jim Carthew.

Altogether they were a clean-bred, self-contained, easy-going band, unostentatious but quietly exclusive—thoroughly representative of the sanest and most reputable section of that variegated cosmos which represents what Gallic students of British sociology term "Le Higlif." Very few of them possessed much money: theirs was a stratum of society to which money was no passport. You could have money if you liked, they conceded, but you must have a good many other things first. Hence the absence from their midst of Hoggenheimer and Aspasia.

Jim Carthew had not meant to come. Juggernaut had given him six weeks' leave, for there had been an Autumn Session in town and an industrial upheaval in the country, and the squire had worked early and late by his knight's side. Consequently when the spring came Carthew was summarily bidden to go to Scotland and fish. Without quite knowing why, he went to Cannes instead, where Nina Tallentyre, attended by a zealous but mutually-distrustful guard-of-honour, was enjoying herself after her fashion under the inadequate wing of Lady Hilton. When the exodus to Algiers was mooted, Carthew labelled his portmanteau London. But he ultimately crossed the Mediterranean with the rest. He had never seen Africa, he explained to himself.

Daphne was of the party too. (Possibly the reader has already identified her as one of the three grass widows.) She had despatched Master Brian Vereker Carr to Belton for a season, and joined the Hiltons' party four weeks ago. The great new house in town stood empty. After her husband's bombshell in February, she had felt bound to do something to show her spirit. Another strike was brewing in the north, so doubtless her lord and master would soon be congenially occupied in starving his dependents into submission. Meanwhile her duty was to herself. Domestic ties were at an end. She would enjoy life.

She experienced no difficulty in the execution of this project. Every one seemed anxious to assist her. Despite precautions, the fact that all was not well in the house of Juggernaut was public property; and the usual distorted rumours on the subject had set out upon their rounds, going from strength to strength in the process. Daphne was soon made conscious that people were sorry for her. Frivolous but warm-hearted women were openly sympathetic. Large, clumsy men indicated by various awkward and furtive acts of kindness that they too understood the situation, but were too tactful to betray the fact. Altogether Daphne was in a fair way to becoming spoiled. With all her faults no one had ever yet been able or inclined to call her anything but unaffected and natural; but about this time she began to assume the virtuous and long-suffering demeanour of a *femme incomprise*. She was only twenty-four, and few of us are able to refuse a martyr's crown when it is pressed upon us.

Only her monosyllabic host—"The Silent Knight," his friends called him, denying him his baronetcy in their zest for the nickname—was unable to appreciate the extreme delicacy of the situation. He was a plain man, Arthur Hilton, and hated mysteries.

"Why isn't that girl at home, lookin' after her husband, Ethel?" he inquired of his wife one morning.

"I think she is happier with us, dear," replied Lady Hilton with immense solemnity.

The Silent Knight emitted a subdued rumble, indicative of a desire to argue the point, and continued—

"Happier—eh? Hasn't she got a baby, or somethin', somewhere? What the dev——"

"Yes, dear, she *has* a baby," replied his wife, rolling up her fine eyes to the ceiling; "but I fear she has not been very fortunate in her marriage. She was the daughter of a country clergyman—*dreadfully* poor, I understand—and wanted to improve the family fortunes. There were eight or nine of them, so she took this old man."

The Silent Knight's engine fairly raced.

"Old man be damned!" he observed with sudden heat. "Sorry, my dear! But Jack Carr can't be more than forty-six. I'm forty-eight. I'm an old man, too, I suppose! Back number—eh? One foot in the grave! You lookin' about for my successor, Ethel—what?"

It was useless to explain to this obtuse and uxorious critic that a young and sensitive girl cannot be expected to dwell continuously beneath the roof of a husband whose tastes are not her tastes, who has merely married her to keep house for him, and who neglects her into the bargain. Not that this prevented Lady Hilton from endeavouring to do so. When she had finished, her husband knocked the ashes out of his pipe, and remarked—

"Can't make you women out. Here's old Juggernaut—best man *I* ever came across, and as kind as they make 'em—marries this little fool of a girl and gives her everything she wants; and she goes off and leaves him slavin' at his work, while she comes trapesin' about here with a collection of middle-aged baby-snatchers and knock-kneed loafers. Next thing, she'll start flirting; then she'll fall in love with some bounder, and then there'll be the devil of a mess. Rotten, I call it! Don't know what wives are comin' to nowadays. Have *you* goin' off next, Ethel—leavin' me and the kids, and becomin' a Suffragette—what?"

After this unusual outburst the Silent Knight throttled himself down and said no more, all efforts on his wife's part to lure him into ground less favourable to his point of view proving fruitless. He merely smoked his pipe and emitted an obstinate purr.

"But what else can one expect, dearest," Ethel Hilton confided to a friend afterwards, "if one marries an internal combustion engine?"

II.

Neither was Mrs Carfrae satisfied to find her beloved Johnny Carr's lawful wife disporting herself in her present company. One afternoon she heckled Jim Carthew upon the subject, to the extreme embarrassment of that loyal youth. The rest of the party had gone off to explore Algiers, and were safely occupied for the present with the contemplation of the passing show— ghostlike Moors in snowy burnouses, baggy-trousered members of that last resort of broken men, *La Légion Étrangère*, and spectacled French officials playing at colonies.

Mrs Carfrae's chair had been wheeled into a corner of the open courtyard which occupied the middle of the Hôtel Magnifique, as far as possible from the base of operations of a pseudo-Tzigane orchestra which discoursed languorous melody twice daily; and its occupant was dispensing to Carthew what Thémistocle was accustomed to describe as "some five o'clock."

"So you are leaving us, Mr Carthew," observed the hostess.

"Yes, the day after to-morrow. There is a boat then. I must go. There is trouble brewing in the colliery districts again, and Sir John wants me."

"And you will take Lady Carr with you?"

"Oh no," said Carthew, flushing. "We are not together. I mean, it is not on her account that I am here."

"So I have noticed," said Mrs Carfrae dryly.

"I was invited here by the Hiltons," explained Carthew, and plunged into a sea of unnecessary corroborative details. "I was quite surprised to find Lady Carr here," he colluded. "I thought she was in London."

"And why," inquired the old lady with sudden ferocity, "is she not at Belton, with her man?"

The faithful Carthew stiffened at once.

"I expect Sir John sent her out here to have a good time," he said. "He could not get away himself, so——"

Mrs Carfrae surveyed him for a moment over her glasses.

"You are a decent lad," she observed rather unexpectedly.

This testimonial had its desired effect of reducing Carthew to silence, and Mrs Carfrae continued—

"You have been with John Carr for some time now, have you not?"

"Yes; ever since I came down from Cambridge."

"How did you meet him? He does not take to young men readily as a rule, so I have heard."

"I had the luck," said Carthew, his eye kindling with historic reminiscence, "to meet him at dinner one night at the end of my third year, at my tutor's. Sir John was an old member of the College, staying there for the week-end. He told us at dinner that he had come up to find a good ignorant unlicked cub to help him with his work, who could be trusted to obey an order when he received one and act for himself when he did not. Those were his exact words, I remember."

"Ay, they would be. Go on."

"This unlicked cub was to come and be a sort of general factotum to him, and do his best to help him with his work, and so on. Marvyn (the tutor) and I sat trying to think of likely men, and finally we made a list of about six, whom Sir John said he would run his eye over next day. After that I went off to bed. I remember wishing to myself that I had taken a better degree and been a more prominent member of the College: then I might have had a shot for this berth, instead of going into a solicitor's office. But as things were, I hadn't the cheek. Well, do you know, Jug—Sir John came round to me next morning——"

"Before breakfast, I doubt."

"Yes, as a matter of fact I had just come in from a run and was sitting down to it. He asked if he might have some: and after that he offered me— ME!—this grand billet. Of course I jumped at it—who wouldn't, to be with a man like that?—and I have been with him ever since."

"Well," said Mrs Carfrae, "you should know more of the creature than most folk. What is your unbiassed opinion of him?"

"I think he is the greatest man that ever lived," said the boy simply.

"Hmph! As a matter of fact, he has less sense than anybody I ever knew," replied the old lady calmly. "Still, you are entitled to your opinion. I need not trouble you with an account of *my* first meeting with him: it occurred a long time ago. But—wheel me a little nearer the sun, laddie: this corner is a thing too shady—it may interest you to know that he would have been my son-in-law to-day, had it not been—" she paused for a moment, very slightly—"for the uncertainty of human life. And that is why I take something more than a passing interest in the doings of that slim-bodied, brown-eyed, tow-headed hempie that he married on. And that brings me to the point. Laddie, those two are getting over-far apart, and it must be *stopped!*"

"Yes, but how?" inquired Carthew dismally. "I understand that entering a lions' den just before dinner-time is wisdom itself compared with interfering between husband and wife."

A quiver passed through Elspeth Carfrae's frail body, and she straightened herself in her chair.

"I am a havering and doited old woman," she announced with great decision, "and no one takes any notice of what I say or do. But I tell you this. So long as my old heart beats and my old blood runs, I shall be perfectly willing to face every single lion in the Zoo, gin it will bring a moment's happiness to Johnny Carr. The lad deserves a good wife. Once he nearly got one—the best and fairest in all the world—but God decided otherwise. Now he has got another: I know her: she has the right stuff in her. And when I leave this hotel next week I am going to take her with me, in her right mind, and deliver her to her man!"

The old lady concluded her intimation with tremendous vigour. Carthew sat regarding her with a mixture of reverence and apprehension.

"You are going to—to speak to her about it?" he asked.

"I am," replied Mrs Carfrae, with vigour.

"I would do anything," said Carthew awkwardly, "to put things right between those two. But supposing you make your attempt, Mrs Carfrae, and—and fail, won't it make matters worse?"

"Much," said Mrs Carfrae calmly. "If I interfere, unsuccessfully, I doubt if either of them will ever speak to me again. That is the usual and proper fate of busybodies. But—I am going to risk it!... Run me back to my sitting-room now, and call Janet. I hear your friends yattering out there in the verandah. They will be through with Algiers."

CHAPTER FIFTEEN.

JIM CARTHEW.

But our two conspirators were fated, for all practical purposes, to exchange *rôles*.

The following evening Daphne and Carthew found themselves sitting together in the hotel garden after dinner. A great moon shone from a velvety African sky; the scented breeze rustled in the palms; and the music of the band drifted to their ears in intermittent waves.

It was one of those nights which touch the imagination and stir the emotions—a night upon which human nature expands to its utmost limits. A night upon which passion awakes, and long-cherished secrets are whispered into suddenly receptive ears. Also a night upon which the devil stalks abroad. Dido resided a few miles from this spot. It was probably a night like this that made the Fourth Book of the Æneid worth writing.

If Dido failed to resist such environment, what of Daphne? She was young; she was intensely susceptible to such things as moonshine and soft music; and, disguise the fact from herself as she might, she was lonely. It is not altogether surprising that, as she surveyed this silent comely youth who lolled beside her eyeing the glittering Mediterranean in stolid abstraction, she should unconsciously have acquiesced in the first of the dismal prognostications of that splenetic but clear-sighted baronet, Sir Arthur Hilton. Jim Carthew had occupied Daphne's thoughts a good deal of late, and to-night she felt suddenly conscious of a desire to flirt with him.

"Cigarette, please!" she commanded.

Carthew silently handed her his case, and allowed her to select and light her own cigarette—a prodigal waste of opportunity, as any professional philanderer could have told her.

"A penny for your thoughts!" continued Daphne pertly.

Carthew, struck by a peculiar note in her voice, turned and looked at her. He was met by a provocative glance. There was a brief silence. Then he said gravely—

"I don't think you are quite cut out for that sort of thing, Lady Carr."

Daphne, feeling as if she had received a whip-lash in the face, stared at him, white with anger. Then she rose stiffly from her seat and moved towards the hotel. Carthew did not stir.

"Don't go," he said. "We may as well have this out."

Daphne stood irresolute. Then curiosity got the better of virtuous indignation, and she sat down again.

"Will you kindly tell me," she said, "what you mean by talking in that way?"

Carthew's honest eyes lingered on her face in a manner which she could not fathom. Did the man love her, or was he pitying her, or was he merely indulging in sarcastic reflections at her expense? Whatever his motives, he had a knack of compelling attention.

Presently he began to speak.

"I wonder," he said, as if talking to himself, "why men and women are made as they are? Why does A love B, while B worships C, who cares for no one in the world but himself? And why does D insist on confusing things still further by not quite knowing what he—she—wants? I wonder! They say there is enough money spent in charity every year to supply the needs of every poor person living, but so much is misapplied that many have to go without. I think it is the same with human affection. There is so much true love going about in this world—enough to keep all of us well-nourished and contented. But what a lot of it goes to waste! There is so much overlapping! *Why*, I wonder? It is a difficult business, Life, Daphne."

He had never called her Daphne before, but neither of them seemed to notice the familiarity.

"We're a contrary crew, we mortals," he continued presently. "Here we are, you and I, sitting in the moonshine inaugurating a flirtation, though neither of us cares a snap for the other—in that way. Why, I wonder? I think it is partly due to pride—wounded pride. You are angry with your husband——"

Daphne, who was methodically picking her cigarette to pieces, looked up indignantly.

"I'm *not*!" she said hotly.

"Oh yes, you are," replied Carthew. "You think you are not, but you are. You try to believe that you are merely indifferent to him, but you are not. As for me, I am angry too—piqued—furious—jealous—raging—I admit it—with a girl whom I dislike intensely. The more I see of her the more selfish, affected, shallow, unwomanly I see her to be. And yet—I *love* her! Why? Why? Why? People tell me she is heartless, soulless, sordid, greedy, vulgar—everything, in fact. Sometimes I feel they are right. Still—" he dropped his head into his hands and continued doggedly—"what difference does that make to *me*? I love her!... She cared for me once, too. She told me so—and she meant it! Perhaps if I had been a little more patient with her I might have kept her, and—and helped her a bit. Perhaps that was what I was sent into the world for—to make things easier for Nina. I could have done so much for her, too. I could have made a woman of her. She has her soft side: I know: I have seen it. No other man can say that. Meanwhile," he continued with a whimsical smile, "I am trying to solace myself by allowing you to flirt with me——"

Daphne drew her breath sharply.

"And you are not very good at it," concluded Carthew unexpectedly.

"You are very candid," said Daphne frigidly.

"Yes, but I speak truth. You are not good at it. Flirtation is a crooked business, and you are straight, *mon amie*. But wounded pride is not the only thing that has drawn us here together. Something else is responsible. We are both craving for sympathy. 'A fellow-feeling,' you know! I know all about *you*," he continued quickly, as Daphne's lips parted. "You are by way of being a neglected wife; and since Nina has informed me that she has told you all about *me*, I suppose you regard me as a bit of a derelict too. Well, we have forgathered. What is going to happen next?"

Daphne was silent. She certainly did not know what was going to happen next. Her ideas on all subjects were a little jumbled at this moment. Presently Carthew continued—

"We came together," he said gently, "just when each of us required a little companionship and sympathy; and we got it. I think our chance encounter on the highway of life has been a very profitable one. But it has served its turn. Our roads diverge again. We must part company, little comrade."

"Why?"

Daphne spoke this time in a tremulous whisper. A great wave of loneliness was surging up towards her.

"Because," said Carthew's deep voice, "it is the only thing to do. Think what may happen if we travel on together too far. At present we are safe. I love some one else, and so do—and you are angry with some one else, let us say. Supposing, since the girl I love does not love me any more—supposing I ceased to love her? It seems hopeless, incredible, I admit; but it might conceivably happen. And supposing you gave up being angry with—some one else, and became indifferent to him, where might we not find ourselves? Our sheet-anchor—our platonic sheet-anchor—would be gone.

And sooner than send you adrift among cross-currents, little Daphne, I prefer to forgo the only friendship in this world that I really value. You are too delicate and too fragrant to be tarnished by common gossip, so I am going away to-morrow. Let us say good-bye now—you beautiful thing!"

Daphne looked up at him in amazement. But there was no passion in his face—only an infinite tenderness. To him she was simply a woman—one of the rarest and fairest of her sex, perhaps, but still simply a woman—whom to succour, without expectation or desire of reward, was the merest courtesy on the part of any knight worthy of the name. This was a man! Daphne bowed her head, wondering dimly and scornfully at the insensate folly of Nina Tallentyre.

"Shall we go back to the hotel?" asked Carthew at length.

There was no reply. Turning to note the cause, he saw something bright and glistening fall upon his companion's hand—then another. With innate loyalty and delicacy he averted his gaze, and surveyed the distant seascape with laborious intentness.

Meanwhile Daphne sat on, her head still bowed. Through the night air, from the hotel verandah, there came the refrain of a waltz. It was called *Caressante*, she thought. Carthew knew it too, and dug his teeth into his lower lip. Waltzes have an unfortunate habit of reviving the memories of yester year.

"Don't go in," said Daphne at length. "Don't leave me—I can't bear it!" Her voice broke.

Suddenly Carthew turned to her.

"Daphne"—his voice was low, but he spoke with intense earnestness—"you are lonely, I know, and sad; and you are too proud to own it. Shall I tell you who is more lonely and more sad, and too proud to own it too?"

"Do you mean—" were Jim Carthew's good resolutions crumbling?—"yourself?"

"No, no,—nothing of the kind. I mean—your husband!" Then he continued hurriedly—

"Daphne, if I thought I was leaving you to real loneliness and inevitable wretchedness, I—well, perhaps I shouldn't go away at all. But I—I am not needed. Little friend, you have the finest husband in all the world, waiting for you. For all his domineering ways, he is shy, and wants knowing. You have never discovered that. I don't believe you know him a bit. It all comes of having begun wrong. Go back and study him. Give him a fair chance! Give yourself a fair chance! You and I have always been friends: will you promise me this? Go back, and give yourself and Jack Carr another chance."

Half an hour ago Daphne would have smiled sceptically and indulgently upon such a suggestion. But this lonely, loyal spirit had touched her. She felt she would like to please him.

"Very well," she said. "I promise. No, *I can't!*" The memory of some ancient wrong suddenly surged up in her, swamping the generous impulse. "*I can't!*"

"Why?"

"Jack is so hard," she said. "Look at the way he treats those in his power. His workpeople, his——"

Carthew laughed, positively boisterously.

"Hard? Jack Carr hard? Listen," he said, "and I will tell you a secret."

When he had finished Daphne stood up, white and gleaming in the moonlight, and gave him her hand.

"All right," she said softly—"it's a bargain. I go home to-morrow."

BOOK THREE.

THE LIGHTING OF THE CANDLE.

CHAPTER SIXTEEN.

SOME ONE TO CONFIDE IN.

Certainly matters were in a serious state in the Mirkley Colliery district. The whole industrial world was unsettled at the time. There had been trouble on the railways, and a great shipyard strike was threatening in Scotland. Most serious of all, the men were beginning to defy their own leaders. They had taken to organising little sectional revolts of their own, and Employers' Federations were beginning to ask how they could be expected to ratify treaties with Trades Union officials who were unable to hold their own followers to the terms of agreements concluded on their behalf.

The Mirkley district had caught the infection. The mischief had originated at Marbledown and Cherry Hill, the immediate cause of the trouble being a simple question of weights and measures.

The ordinary collier is paid by piecework—so much per ton for all the coal he hews. This coal is carefully weighed on coming to the surface, and to ensure fair play all round the weight is checked by the men's own representative at the pit-head. Now just as all is not gold that glitters, so all that comes to the surface of the earth from the interior of a coal-pit is not necessarily coal. A good deal of it is shale, stone, and the like—technically summarised as "dirt"—and has to be sorted out from the genuine article by a bevy of young ladies retained at some expense for the purpose. As colliers are paid for hewing coal and not dirt, the mine managers, reckoning one hundredweight as the average weight of dirt in a tub of coal, had been in the habit, when making out their pay-sheets, of deducting this amount from the total weight of each load brought to the surface. *Hinc lacrymæ.* The man in the pit claimed that he should be paid for all he sent up the shaft, alleging that it was impossible to separate coal from dirt at the face, and that dirt was quite as difficult to hew as coal. To this those in authority replied that a collier is a man who is employed to hew coal and not dirt, and that as such he should only be paid for the coal he hewed. It was a nice point, and so high did feeling run upon the subject, and so fierce was the demeanour of their *employés,* that pliable Mr Aymer and pusillanimous Mr Montague yielded to the extent of fifty-six pounds, and henceforth each toiler in Cherry Hill and Marbledown Colliery was debited with one half instead of one whole hundredweight of dirt per tub.

Encouraged by the success of their colleagues, the men employed at Sir John Carr's great pit at Belton proffered a similar request. But though the request was the same its recipient was different. Sir John greeted the deputation with disarming courtesy, and announced in a manner which precluded argument that on the question of the owners' right to deduct for dirt in each load he would not yield one inch. On this the deputation rashly changed their ground and alleged that the toll of one hundredweight per tub was excessive. Whereupon Juggernaut whisked them off without delay to the pit-head. Here a minute examination was made of the contents of the next ten tubs of coal which came to the surface, and it was found that, so far from defrauding his *employés*, Juggernaut was defrauding himself, for the average weight of dirt in each tub was not one hundred and twelve but one hundred and thirty pounds.

"You see, Mr Brash?" said Sir John cheerfully. "I am afraid you have all been in my debt to the extent of eighteen pounds of coal per tub for quite a considerable number of years. However, if you will be sensible and go back to work, we will call it a wash-out and say no more about it."

Then he departed to London.

But he had to return. The half-hundredweight of Cherry Hill and Marbledown outbalanced Belton's plain facts and ocular demonstrations. The Pit "came out" *en masse*, against the advice and without the authority of their Union officials; and for two or three weeks men loafed up and down the long and unlovely street which comprised Belton village, smoking their pipes and organising occasional whippet-races against the time when the despot who employed them should be pleased to open negotiations.

But the despot made no sign. Presently pipes were put away for want of tobacco, and whippet-racing ceased for want of stake-money. Then came a tightening of belts and a setting of teeth, and men took to sitting on their heels against walls and fences, punctuating recrimination by expectoration, through another four long and pitiful weeks.

Not so utterly pitiful though. For a wonderful thing happened. The unknown benefactor of the strike of seven years ago came to life again. Every morning the postman delivered to the wife of each man in Belton a packet containing a ration of tea, sugar, and (once a week) bacon. Coal, too, was distributed by a mysterious motor-lorry, bearing a London number-plate, and manned by two sardonic Titans, who deposited their sacks and answered no questions. So there was no actual destitution in the village. But there was no beer, and no tobacco, and no money. Women and children can live for an amazingly long time on tea and sugar eked out by a little bread, but man is the slave of an exacting stomach, and requires red meat for the upkeep of his larger frame. The whippets, too, had to be considered; and when, after an interval of seven weeks, a notice went up on the gates of the pit buildings, intimating that all who returned to work on the following Monday would be reinstated without question, Belton Colliery put its pride into its empty pocket and came back as one man.

But the danger was not over yet, as Juggernaut well knew. For the moment the men were subdued by sheer physical exhaustion. The first pay-day would fill their bellies and put some red blood into their passions. And it was certain information, received on this head at the Pit offices, that sent Sir John Carr home to Belton Hall with knitted brow and tight-set mouth one wintry Saturday afternoon in early April, a fortnight after the men had resumed work.

He stepped out of the big motor and walked into the cheerful fire-lit hall. He stood and gazed reflectively upon the crackling logs as the butler removed his heavy coat. But the removal of the coat seemed to take no weight from his shoulders. He felt utterly lonely and unhappy. Was he growing old, he wondered. He was not accustomed to feel like this. He did not usually shrink from responsibility, or desire a shoulder to lean upon, but at this moment he suddenly felt the want of some one to consult. No; consult was not the word! He could have consulted Carthew. In fact he had just done so, for Carthew had returned from his holiday two days before. What he wanted was some one to *confide* in. With a sudden tightening of the heart he thought of a confidante who might have been at his side then, had things been different—a confidante who would have sat upon the arm of his chair and bidden him play the man and fear nothing. Well, doubtless he would play the man and fear nothing, and doubtless he would win again as he had done before. But—*cui bono*? What doth it profit a man——?

He wondered where she was. Yachting on the Mediterranean, or frivolling on the Riviera. Or perhaps she was back in London by this time, ordering her spring clothes and preparing for another butterfly season. At any rate she was not at Belton Hall. Whose fault was that?...

Had he been lacking in patience with her? Had he treated her too much like a refractory board-meeting?... A little fool? Doubtless; but then, so were most women. And she was very young, after all....

"Will you take anything before dinner, sir?" inquired a respectful voice in his ear. "Tea? Whisky-and——"

"No, thank you, Graves. Is Master Brian in the nursery?"

"Yes, sir."

"I will go up shortly and say good-night to him. Meanwhile I shall be in the study if Mr Carthew or any one calls for me. But I don't want to be disturbed at present."

A minute later he opened the door of the apartment, half library, half smoking-room, which he called his study. It was in darkness, but for the cheerful glow of the fire.

As Juggernaut closed the door behind him and felt for the electric-light switch, there came a rustling from the depths of a great oak settle which formed a right-angle with the projecting mantelpiece; and a slim straight figure stood suddenly upright, silhouetted against the ruddy glare.

"Daphne!"

"Yes—me!" replied an extremely small voice.

CHAPTER SEVENTEEN.

THE CANDLE LIT.

There is no more disagreeable sensation in this world than that furnished by a sudden encounter with some one with whom we are on "awkward" terms. Most people know what it is to cross the street to avoid an old friend, or to dodge into a shop in order to escape the necessity of inflicting or receiving the cut direct. Very often the origin of the quarrel has been forgotten or ceased to be of real moment, but the awkwardness endures. Oftener still a reconciliation would be welcomed on both sides; but pride, pride, pride intervenes.

Now the best solvent of stubborn obstinacy is a sense of humour. As Juggernaut stood in the darkness, surveying the embarrassed little figure before him—in his eyes Daphne, five feet seven in her stockings, was always "little"—and feeling acutely conscious on his own part of an irresistible desire to shuffle with his feet, he suddenly and most providentially broke into one of his rare laughs—a laugh of quiet and unforced enjoyment.

Apparently this was not quite what Daphne expected.

"What is the matter?" she inquired. Her voice quavered pathetically, for she was highly wrought.

"I couldn't help thinking," said her husband, "of an episode in the history of two old friends of mine. They had been engaged for about three months, when they quarrelled—severely. They parted company for ever, and whenever he or she saw the other upon the horizon, he or she fled. However, after about six weeks of this sort of thing they were taken by surprise. One day the man saw the girl advancing straight upon him down the street, quite oblivious of his proximity. He dived into the nearest shop, which happened to be a baby-linen establishment—"

Daphne gave a sudden gurgle of laughter.

"—And when the girl walked in, two minutes later," concluded Juggernaut, "to match some silk, she found her late beloved diligently sampling Berlin wool. That did it! The sense of humour of that young couple came to their rescue, Daphne, and they walked out of the shop hand-in-hand, not caring a dump for anybody. To my knowledge they have never had a quarrel since. You see the reason why I laughed just now?"

Daphne sighed comfortably.

"Yes," she said. The tension of the situation was relaxed.

"I want to—to talk to you, Jack," she continued, considerably heartened.

"Certainly," replied Juggernaut, with a slight return of his board-room air. "I'll turn the light on."

"Please don't," said Daphne hastily. "I would rather talk in the dark. Will you sit down on the settle?"

Juggernaut obeyed silently. The firelight played upon his face, showing the clear-cut lines of his mouth and his tired eyes. Daphne stood erect before him, keeping her face in the shadow. She had removed her hat and furs, and her thick hair caught the light fantastically.

"Jack," she began, industriously scrutinising the vista of the room reflected by an ancient convex mirror hanging on the far wall, "I want to say something. I want to say that I am sorry. I have done you an injustice. I always thought you were a hard man, and I have discovered that you are not. In fact," she continued with a flicker of a smile, "I have found out that you are very much the other thing." She paused.

"May I ask for chapter and verse?" said Juggernaut.

"*Yes!*" The old Daphne flashed forth. "Here are you, fighting all these men with one hand, giving no quarter, and all that sort of thing—" Juggernaut stirred suddenly in his seat—"and feeding the women and children with the other! Aren't you, now?" She pointed an accusing finger.

"Since you tax me with it—yes," said her husband.

Daphne turned upon him impulsively, with the firelight full on her face.

"Jack," she said softly, "it was splendid of you!"

He looked up and saw that her eyes were glowing. She came a step nearer, and her head drooped prettily. "And I'm sorry if I have been unfair to you, Jack," she continued. "I—I thought you were just a feelingless sort of man, whose work was his world, and who cared for nothing but himself and what he had in view, and regarded women as merely useful things to keep house, and have babies, and so on. But now I *know* that I was wrong. There is more of you than that. Being me, I had to tell you."

She ended with a little catch in her voice. She had made her effort. She had humbled herself, and in so doing she had laid herself open to the cruellest of rebuffs. She waited tremulously. A hard word, a scornful smile, even silence now—and two lives would fall asunder for ever.

But the wheels of Juggernaut had never passed over a woman.

"Will you sit down?" said Sir John gently.

He made room for her, and she sank down beside him, leaning her head against the high back of the settle and gazing unwinkingly into the fire. She was conscious now that this man was overflowing with tenderness towards her, but she would not look him in the face yet.

"How did you find out about the rations to the women?" he enquired presently.

Daphne told him.

"But you mustn't blame Jim Carthew," she said in conclusion. "He simply *had* to tell me."

"Where did you see him?"

"Last week, in Algiers. In fact, he brought me home; but I made him promise not to tell you I was in London. He *is* a good sort!" she added irrelevantly.

"In what way?" asked her husband curiously.

Daphne turned and surveyed him.

"Would you be angry if I told you—jealous, I mean?"

"What right have I to be angry or jealous?" said Juggernaut simply. "In what way," he repeated, "has Carthew been showing that he is a good sort?"

"Well, in bringing me his troubles. That always makes a conquest of any woman, you know. And in letting me take my troubles to him. A woman always *has* to take a trouble to a man, Jack, when all is said and done—even if he is only the family solicitor!" she concluded hurriedly. She had suddenly skated on to thin ice, and she knew it. The man to whom she should have taken her troubles had not been there to receive them.

"So Jim Carthew has his troubles like the rest of us?" said Juggernaut.

"Yes, and I never suspected how he felt about them," said Daphne. "He is fearfully reserved about the things he really feels, although he babbles enough about the things he doesn't. So, when I was in trouble——"

"What was your trouble?"

"I was lonely," said the girl.

Juggernaut drew his breath sharply.

"I am glad you had some one to be kind to you," he said.

Then came a long pause—the sort of pause which either brings a discussion to an end or begets another, longer and more intimate. We all know them.

Finally Daphne braced herself.

"Jack," she said, "I want to say something more. I didn't mean to: I have said all I came here to say. But I must say this too—now or never. I—I—I was wrong to marry you, Jack. I didn't love you, but I thought it didn't matter. I felt how divine it would be to be able to help the boys and Dad. That was all I considered. Then, when I began to go about, and meet new people, and make comparisons, I—found myself criticising you! *Me—you!*"

"I wouldn't be too indignant about it if I were you," said her husband.

He reached out deliberately for her hand, and continued his contemplation of the fire.

"Go on," he said.

Daphne, foolishly uplifted, continued—

"I used to think you rough and hard and unsympathetic. I began to prefer the men who buzzed round and murmured things in my ear. And when people began to pity me as a neglected wife, I—I encouraged them. I let women say catty things about you, and I let men make love to me. That sort of thing has been going on ever since the time"—Daphne's grip of her husband's hand tightened—"when you and I decided—to go our own ways. I don't mind telling you now that it was a pill for me, Jack. My pride——"

"It was a brutal act on my part," blazed out Juggernaut with sudden passion.

"No it *wasn't*: it was what I deserved!" insisted Daphne, whose nature did not permit her to be repentant by halves. "Well, anyhow, I determined to flirt in real earnest now. So I began to carry on in an experimental fashion. But I can't say it was much fun. Finally I did fall in love with a man, in a sort of way—don't hurt my hand, dear; it was only in a sort of way—and I let him see it. Well, I got a facer over *him*. One night, under the moon, I tried to flirt with him; and he—well, Jack, he fairly put me in my place!"

"What did he do?"

"He made me feel ashamed of myself."

"What did he say?"

"Not much that we need talk of now, except one thing."

"What was that?"

"He told me to go back to you."

"Why?"

"Because he said"—Daphne's voice dropped low—"that you loved me."

There was a long silence, until a live coal subsided in the grate. Then Juggernaut said—

"It was Carthew, I suppose."

Daphne nodded.

"Jack," she said, "Jim Carthew is the best friend that you and I possess."

"I know it."

They were silent again, until irrelevant Daphne enquired suddenly—

"Jack, what made you do that unpractical thing? The tea and sugar, I mean. It was only prolonging the strike: even *I* can see that."

"It didn't prolong the strike to any particular extent," said Juggernaut with decision. "Not that I care," he added with unusual inconsequence, "if it did. It made things no easier for the men; and it is with the men that the decision lies in cases of this kind."

"But it was so *unlike* you," persisted Daphne.

Her husband turned and regarded her quizzically.

"Was it?" he said, smiling. "We all have our weaknesses," he added. "Mine are women and children. I think," he went on with great deliberation, "that there is only one woman in this wide world who has ever suffered ill at my hands."

"And she is——"

"My wife! Listen," he continued rapidly, "while I make confession. You have spoken your piece bravely, Daphne. Now hear me mine."

He rose in his turn, and stood before his wife.

"I never knew or cared very much about women," he said. "I do not remember my mother, and I had no sisters, which probably accounts for a good deal. Also, I was brought up by a man among men, and I learned to read men and handle men to the exclusion of all else. I was given to understand that women did not matter. I was trained to regard them as a sort of inferior and unreliable variety of the male sex. So I confined my dealings to men, and I found so much joy in handling and mastering men that my eyes became closed to the fact that life could offer me anything else."

"But didn't you miss female society? Most men can't get on without *some*," said experienced Daphne.

"You can't miss what you have never had, little girl. Perhaps if I had encountered female society early in life——"

"But didn't you sometimes instinctively long for a woman to come and take charge of you? Most men are so helpless and messy by themselves."

"Sometimes," admitted Juggernaut almost reluctantly, "I did. But I put the notion from me."

"Shall I tell you why?" said Daphne quietly.

"I suppose it was because I didn't want to yield to a weakness."

"It was nothing of the kind," said Daphne with immense decision. "It was because you were *afraid*!"

"Afraid?"

"Yes—afraid! You would have nothing to do with women, because you told yourself you despised them. We were a waste of time, you said—an encumbrance! The real reason was that you feared us. Yes—feared! Success was the breath of life to you. You had always had your own way wherever you went. You were the great Sir John Carr—the strong man—Juggernaut! You had never been beaten. Why? Because you had never had the pluck to try conclusions with a woman. Your excuse was that you were a woman-hater, when all the time you were a woman-lover. You have just admitted it, impostor! You were afraid that where every man had failed to turn you from your own hard selfish way of life, a woman might succeed. And so you ran away, and you have been running ever since. There, my strong man, there's the truth for you!"

For once in his life Sir John Carr, the terror of deputations, the scourge of unsound logicians, the respectfully avoided of hecklers, had no answer ready. The reason was obvious: no answer was possible. The victory lay with Daphne. She leaned back in the settle and looked fearlessly up into her husband's face. For the first time in her life she felt maternal towards this man—twenty-two years her senior—just as old Mrs Carfrae had predicted. She was utterly and absolutely happy, too, for she had just realised that she and her husband had come together at last. They were one flesh. The time for tactful diplomacy and mutual accommodation and making allowances was over-past. No need now to guard the flame from sudden gusts and cross-winds. The candle was safely lighted, and, please God, it should burn steadily to its socket. The Safety Match had accomplished its task after all.

Then she gave a happy little sigh, for her husband's great arm was around her shoulders.

"All my life, Daphne," said his deep voice, "I have thought that the sweetest thing in this world was victory. Now I have just received my first defeat—you routed me, hip and thigh—and I am happier than I have ever been. Why?"

"Think!" commanded a muffled voice in the neighbourhood of his waistcoat.

Juggernaut obeyed. Then he continued, and his grip round Daphne grew stronger—

"I think I see. I married you because I wanted some one to keep my house in order and bear me a son. (That point of view did not endure long, I may say, for I fell in love with you on our honeymoon, and I have loved you ever since; but it was my point of view when I asked you to marry me.) I thought then that it would be a fair bargain if I gave you money and position in return for these things. We could not help living contentedly together, I considered, under the terms of such a logical and business-like contract as that. Well, I did not know then, what I know now, that logic and business are utterly valueless as a foundation for any contract between a man and a woman. The only thing that is the slightest use for the purpose is the most illogical and unbusiness-like thing in the whole wide world. And"—his iron features relaxed into a smile of rare sweetness—"I believe, I believe, *cara mia*, that you and I have found that thing—together." His voice dropped lower. "Have we, Daphne—my wife?"

Daphne raised her head, and looked her man full in the face.

"We have found it, O my husband," she said gravely—"at last!"

———

The door flew open suddenly. There was a gleam of electric light. Graves, the imperturbable, inclined respectfully before them.

"You are wanted outside, sir," he said, "badly!"

CHAPTER EIGHTEEN.

ATHANASIUS CONTRA MUNDUM.

A confused medley of men and women—not to mention the inevitable small boy element—was pouring up the road from Belton Pit in the direction of the Hall, which lay beyond the brow of the hill in a green hollow as yet unsullied by winding-wheels and waste-heaps. People who have made up their minds to do evil are usually in a hurry to get it over. Consequently our friends were advancing at a high rate of speed, keeping up their courage by giving forth unmelodious noises.

Juggernaut's prophecy had come true. The rebellion had been damped down by sheer starvation; and now that starvation was over-past, the rebellion was flaming out again with tenfold vigour. That fine unreasoning human instinct which under a certain degree of pressure bids logic and argument go hang, and impels us to go forth and break some one else's windows, held the reins that evening. As the night-shift assembled at the pit-head, what time the day-shift was being disgorged, a cageful at a time, from the depths below, a great and magnificent project suddenly hatched itself in the fertile brain of Mr Tom Winch, who had been haunting the neighbourhood on business connected with the propaganda of his own particular revolutionary organisation for the past six weeks. Now was his chance. Evil passions, hitherto dimmed by hunger and privation, were reviving. The men were ripe for any mischief. What they were asking for, reflected Mr Winch, was blood, or its equivalent, and a man to lead them to it.

Mr Winch was, to do him justice, a master of his own furtive trade. In five minutes his project was circulating through the throng. In fifteen the crowd had pledged itself to do something really big; and in half an hour most of the windows of the pit offices had been broken as a guarantee of good faith.

Having whetted its appetite on this *hors-d'œuvre*, the mob listened readily to Mr Winch's suggestion of a brisk walk to Belton Hall and a personal interview with its proprietor. The notion ran through the excited mass of humanity like fire through dry grass; and presently, as if from one spontaneous impulse, the advance on Belton Hall began. No one quite knew what he proposed to do when he got there, but the possibilities of the expedition were great. It was a picturesque procession, for every man carried a safety-lamp in one hand and a missile in the other. It was probably owing to the multiplicity of the twinkling points of light thus produced that no one observed the flickering halo of a solitary bicycle-lamp, as the machine which bore it slipped out from the side-door of the pit offices and silently stole away through the darkness, carrying a frightened messenger over the hill to Belton Hall.

It may here be noted that Mr Tom Winch, having despatched his avenging host upon its way, remained behind at headquarters—doubtless to superintend the subsequent operations with that degree of perspective which is so necessary to a good general. Mr Killick, an old acquaintance of ours, supported by his friend Mr Brash, led the procession.

"Supposin' the lodge gates is locked—what then?" enquired Mr Brash— ever a better critic than creator of an enterprise—as they trudged along the muddy road.

"We shall trample them down," replied Mr Killick, ever contemptuous of irritating detail.

But the lodge gates stood hospitably open. The lodge itself was shuttered and silent; and the procession, pausing momentarily to deliver a hilarious and irregular volley of small coal, proceeded on its way.

Up the long avenue they tramped. There were electric lamps at intervals, intended for the guidance of strange coachmen on dinner-party nights. These were all ablaze. Evidently Juggernaut was expecting friends.

Five minutes later our glorious company of apostles rounded the last turn in the avenue, and the broad Elizabethan *façade* of Belton Hall loomed up before them. Every window was alight.

A flagged and balustraded terrace ran along the whole frontage of the Hall. In the middle of the balustrade was a gap, where a broad flight of shallow stone steps led down to a velvety lawn three hundred years old. Most of the crowd knew that lawn and terrace well. The grounds at Belton were constantly and freely granted for miners' *fêtes*, political demonstrations, and the like. On these occasions a band was nearly always playing upon the terrace, and not infrequently post-prandial orations were outpoured from the rostrum formed by the stone steps upon the heads of a gorged and tolerant audience on the grass below.

To-night no band was playing; but at the head of the steps—motionless, upright, inflexible—stood a solitary figure. It was the master of the house, waiting to receive his guests—one against four hundred.

But to one who knew, the odds were not overwhelming. In fact, provided that the crowd possessed no resolute leader, the chances were slightly in favour of the figure on the steps. One man with his wits about him has two great advantages over a crowd. In the first place, he knows exactly what he is going to do, and, in the second, he knows exactly what the crowd is going to do. The crowd knows neither. It is impossible to foretell how a single individual will behave upon emergency: the human temperament varies too widely. But there is nothing in the world so normal or conventional as a crowd. Mankind in the lump is a mere puppet in the hands of the law of averages. Given, as noted above, a resolute leader, the conditions are changed. The leader imbues the crowd with a portion of his own spirit, and creates an instinct of unanimity. Then the odds are once more in favour of the crowd; for now it is a resolute will, all alone, pitted against a resolute will with force behind it.

Sir John Carr knew all this. He had studied men all his life; and as he stood silent and observant, surveying the surging multitude at his feet—it had flowed to the base of the steps now—he noted that there was no leader in particular. The crowd were acting under the influence of blind impulse, and, if properly handled, could be swayed about and sent home.

Presently the hubbub ceased, and the men stood gazing upward, fingering lumps of coal and waiting for some one to fire the first shot.

"Good evening, ladies and gentlemen," observed Juggernaut. [The ladies, be it noted, constituted the front row of the assemblage, their cavaliers having modestly retired a few paces under their employer's passionless scrutiny.] "If you have come to serenade me, I shall have pleasure presently in sending you out some refreshment. If you have merely come to burn the house down, I strongly advise you to go home and think twice about it."

The recipients of this piece of advice were undoubtedly a little taken aback. Playful badinage was the last thing they had expected. They murmured uneasily one to another, debating suitable retorts. Presently a shrill female voice opened fire.

"Tyrant!"

"Money-grubber!" corroborated another voice.

"Who starves women and children?" shrieked a third.

"Yah! Booh!" roared the crowd, taking heart.

"Chuck some of his own coals at 'im!" was the frantic adjuration of a foolish virgin who had already expended all her ammunition against the shutters of the gate-lodge.

A lump of something black and crystalline sang past Juggernaut's head, and struck a richly glowing stained-glass window twenty feet behind him. There was a sharp crash and a silvery tinkle, followed by a little gasp from the crowd. The first shot had been fired. Juggernaut knew well that a broadside was imminent, and countered swiftly. In the startled silence which succeeded the destruction of the great window—it had lighted the staircase at Belton for generations—his voice rang out like a trumpet.

"Listen to me!" he cried. "You have a grievance. You have come up here to square accounts with me. You think you have right on your side: I think it is on mine. Both of us are spoiling for a fight. In our present frame of mind nothing else will satisfy us. Now here is a fair offer. Send up any two men you like out of that multitude down there, and I will take them on, both together or one after the other, as you please. I am rising forty-seven, but if I fail to drop either of your representatives over this balustrade, back where he came from, inside of five minutes, I promise to remit the dues on that odd hundredweight that you are making all this to do about. Is it a bargain, gentlemen?"

He had struck the right note. The low, angry murmuring suddenly ceased, and a great wave of Homeric laughter rolled over the crowd. The British collier has his faults, but within his limits he is a sportsman. He appreciates pluck.

"Good lad!" roared a voice out of the darkness. Then there fell another silence.

"I am waiting, gentlemen," said Juggernaut presently.

But he had to continue waiting. His audience, as previously noted, were sportsmen within limits. The limits, alas! in those soft days are too often the coursing of a half-blinded rabbit, or the backing of a horse in a race which will not be witnessed by the backer. It is always gratifying to be invited to participate in a sporting event, but there is a difference between a seat on the platform and a stance in the arena. Getting hurt gratuitously is slipping into the *index expurgatorius* of modern field sports.

Men began to look sheepishly at one another. One or two had started forward instinctively, but the impulse died away. A humourist was heard imploring his friends to hold him back. There was something unutterably grim about the towering figure up on the terrace. Democracy and the equality of mankind to the contrary, Jack usually recognises his master when it comes to a pinch. No Jack seemed to desire advancement on this occasion.

Juggernaut waited for another minute. He wanted the silence to sink in. He wanted the crowd to feel ridiculous. That object achieved, he proposed to turn his visitors to the right-about and send them home. He had been through this experience before, and felt comparatively sure of his ground.

Provided, that is, that one thing did not occur. There were women present.

Now women are exempt from the law of averages: the sex snaps its fingers at computations based upon laboriously compiled statistics. If the women—or more likely a woman—gave the men a lead, anything might happen. And just as Juggernaut uplifted his voice to pronounce a valediction, the disaster befel.

"Now go home," he began. "You are not yourselves to-night. Go home, and think things over. Consult the older men: I see none of them here. If you are of the same mind to-morrow, I promise to——"

"Call yourselves men? Cowards! cowards! cowards! One of *us* is worth the lot of you!"

A woman, with a shawl over her head and a child in her arms, had mounted half-way up the steps, and was addressing the mob below. Sir John recognised her as Mrs Brash, a quiet little person as a rule.

"Come up, chaps!" she shrieked. "Are you going to let him stamp on us *all*? Look at his fine house, and his electrics, and his marble steps and all!" [They were plain freestone, but let that pass.] "Where did he get 'em all? From *us*—us that he has starved and clemmed this last two months! Are you afraid of him—the lot of you? Great hulking cowards! I see you, Brash, hiding there! Isn't there *one* man here?"

"Yes—by *God* there is!"

With a bound, Killick, the brooding visionary, the Utopian Socialist, was at the top of the steps, brandishing a pit-prop and haranguing his comrades. There was no stopping him. Mrs Brash had fired the train and Killick was the explosion. His words gushed out—hot, passionate, delirious. The man's sense of proportion, always unstable, was gone entirely. He burned with the conviction of his own wrongs and those of his fellows. *Nobilis ira* gave him eloquence. He laid violent hands upon wealth and power and greed and tyranny, and flung them one by one down the steps on to the heads of his hearers. Most of what he said was entirely irrelevant; a great deal more was entirely untrue; but it served. For the moment Sir John Carr stood for all the injustice and cruelty that strength has ever inflicted upon weakness. Every word told. The mob was aflame at last. They hung upon Killick's fiery sentences, surging ever more closely round the steps. The next wave, Juggernaut saw, would bring them in a flood upon the terrace; and then— what? He thought coolly and rapidly. There was Daphne to consider—also little Brian. Daphne, he knew, was close by, standing with beating heart behind the curtains of the library window. He had forbidden her to come farther. Perhaps, though, she had been sensible, and taken the opportunity of this delay to slip away. Of course, of course.

There was a movement beside him, and he realised that his education in femininity still left something to be desired. A hand slid into his, and Daphne's voice whispered in his ear—

"Jack, I want to speak to them."

Her husband turned and smiled upon her curiously.

"What are you going to say?" he asked.

"I am going to tell them about—about the tea and sugar. It's the only thing to do," said Daphne eagerly.

"I would rather be knocked on the head by a pit-prop!" said Juggernaut. And he meant it. Some of us are terribly afraid of being exposed as sentimentalists.

Meanwhile the crowd had caught sight of Daphne. The men fell silent, as men are fain to do when a slim goddess, arrayed in black velvet, appears to them, silhouetted against a richly glowing window. But there was a vindictive shriek from the women.

"Get back at once, dear," said Juggernaut. "You are in great danger. Telephone to the police, and tell Graves to get the fire-hose out. It may be useful in two ways. I promise to come in if things get worse. Hallo! who is that?"

A burly man in a bowler hat, panting with the unwonted exertion of a two-mile run, was approaching him along the terrace. He had come up the drive unnoticed, and having skirted the edge of the crowd had gained access to the terrace from another flight of steps at the end. It was Mr Walker, the mine manager.

"I tried to get you on the telephone," he shouted in Juggernaut's ear; "but they have cut the wire."

"What is it?" asked Juggernaut.

Walker told him.

There was just time to act. The mob were pouring up the steps in response to Killick's final invitation. Juggernaut strode forward.

"Stop!" he cried in a voice of thunder. "Stop, and listen to what Mr Walker has to tell you!"

His great voice carried, and there was a moment's lull. Walker seized his opportunity.

"There has been an accident at the pit," he bellowed. "Some of your lads went down after you had left, to see what damage they could do to the plant. Some of the older men went down to stop them. Something happened. The roofs of the main road and intake have fallen in, and Number Three Working is cut off—with eight men in it!"

There was a stricken silence, and the wave rolled back from the steps. Presently a hoarse voice cried—

"Who are they?"

Mr Walker recited six names. Four of these belonged to young bloods who had been foremost in the riot at the pit-head. There were agonised cries from women in the crowd. All four men were married. The fifth name, that of Mr Adam Wilkie, who was a bachelor and a misogynist, passed without comment. The sixth was that of a pit-boy named Hopper.

Mr Walker paused.

"You said eight!" cried another woman's voice in an agony of suspense. "The other two—for the love of God!"

"Amos Entwistle," replied Mr Walker grimly—"and Mr Carthew."

CHAPTER NINETEEN.

LABORARE EST ORARE.

Six men sat upon six heaps of small coal in a long rectangular cavern five feet high and six feet broad. The roof was supported by props placed at distances specified by the Board of Trade. One side of the cavern was pierced at regular intervals by narrow openings which were in reality passages; the other was a blank wall of gleaming coal.

This was the "face"—that point in the seam of coal which marked the limits of progress of the ever-advancing line of picks and shovels.

The men were well over two hundred fathoms—roughly a quarter of a mile—below the surface of the earth, and they had been prisoners in Number Three Working ever since an explosion of fire-damp and coal-dust had cut them off from communication with the rest of Belton Pit six hours before.

The prisoners were Jim Carthew, Amos Entwistle, and Adam Wilkie, together with a hewer, a drawer, and a pit-boy, named Atkinson, Denton, and Hopper respectively. There had been two others, but they lay dead and buried beneath a tombstone twelve hundred feet high.

What had happened was this.

About four o'clock on that disastrous afternoon, Amos Entwistle was sitting despondently in his own kitchen. He was the oldest and most influential overman in Belton Pit, but his counsels of moderation had been swept aside by the floods of Mr Winch's oratory; and like the practical creature that he was he had returned home, to await the issue of the insurrection and establish an alibi in the event of police-court proceedings.

To him entered Mr Adam Wilkie, with the news that some of the more ardent iconoclasts of the day-shift had remained below in the pit, in order to break down the roofs of some of the galleries leading to the workings— an amiable and short-sighted enterprise which, though pleasantly irritating to their employer, must inevitably throw its promoters and most of their friends out of work for an indefinite period.

Here at least was an opportunity to act. Entwistle hastily repaired to the pit-offices, where he knew that Mr Carthew had been spending the afternoon; and the three, united for the moment by the bond of common-sense, if nothing else, dropped down the shaft with all speed. Fortunately the man in charge of the winding-engine was still at his post, and of an amenable disposition.

Arrived at the pit bottom, they hurried along the main road. The atmosphere was foul and close, for the ventilating machinery had ceased to work. There was a high percentage of fire-damp, too, as constant little explosions in their Davy lamps informed them.

Presently they overtook the enemy, who had done a good deal of mischief already; for they had set to work in the long tunnel known as the intake, down which fresh air was accustomed to flow to the distant workings; and at every blow of their picks, a pit-prop fell from its position and an overhead beam followed, bringing down with it a mingled shower of stone and rubbish.

There was no time to be lost, for the whole roof might fall at any moment. It was three against five; but authority is a great asset and conscience a great liability. By adopting a "hustling" policy of the most thorough description, Carthew, Entwistle, and Wilkie hounded their slightly demoralised opponents along the intake towards the face, intending to round up the gang in one of the passages leading back to the main road, and, having pursued the policy of peaceful dissuasion to its utmost limits, conduct their converts back to the shaft.

The tide of battle rolled out of the intake into the cavern formed by the face and its approaches. Master Hopper was the first to arrive, the toe of Mr Entwistle's boot making a good second.

"Now, you men," said Carthew, addressing the sullen, panting figures which crouched before him—the roof here was barely five feet above the floor—"we have had enough of this. Get out into the main road and back to the shaft. You are coming up topside of this pit with us—that's flat!"

But his opponents were greater strategists than he supposed.

"Keep them there, chaps!" cried a voice already far down one of the passages.

"Catch that man!" cried Carthew. "Let me go!"

Shaking off Atkinson, who in obedience to orders had made a half-hearted grab at him, he darted down the nearest passage. It led to the main road, but across the mouth hung a wet brattice-cloth. Delayed a moment, he hurried on towards the junction with the main road, just in time to descry two twinkling Davy lamps disappearing round the distant corner. They belonged to Davies and Renwick, the ringleaders of the gang. What their object might be he could not for the moment divine, but he could hear their voices re-echoing down the silent tunnel. Evidently they were making for the main road, perhaps to raid the engine-room or call up reserves. He must keep them in sight. Laboriously he hastened along the rough and narrow track.

Suddenly, far ahead in the darkness, he heard a crash, followed by a frightened shriek. Next moment there was a roar, which almost broke the drums of his ears, and the whole pit seemed to plunge and stagger. His lamp went out, and he lay upon the floor in the darkness—darkness that could be felt—waiting for the roof to fall in.

Renwick and Davies, it was discovered long afterwards, had reached the main road, running rapidly. Here one of them must have tripped over the slack-lying wire cable which drew the little tubs of coal up the incline from the lyes to the foot of the shaft. Two seconds later a tiny puddle of flaming oil from a broken lamp (which for once in a way had not been extinguished by its fall) had supplied the necessary ignition to the accumulated fire-damp and coal-dust of the unventilated pit. There was one tremendous explosion. Down came the roof of the main road for a distance of over half a mile, burying the authors of the catastrophe, Samson-like, in their own handiwork.

The survivors were sitting in the *cul-de-sac* formed by the face of the coal and its approaches, three-quarters of a mile from the shaft. No one had been injured by the explosion, though Carthew, being nearest, had lain half-stunned for a few minutes. Possibly the brattice-cloths hung at intervals across the ways to direct the air-currents had been instrumental in blanketing its force.

The party had just returned from an investigation of the possibilities of escape.

"Will you report, Mr Entwistle?" said Carthew, who found that the surviving mutineers appeared to regard him as the supreme head of the present enterprise and Entwistle as his chief adviser.

Amos Entwistle complied.

There were two ways, he explained in his broad north-country dialect, by which Number Three could be reached from the shaft. One was the intake, along which fresh air was conducted to the workings, and the other was the main road, which could be reached through any of the passages leading away from the face. The explosion in the main road had brought down the roof for a distance which might be almost anything. The intake was blocked too. It was some way from the scene of the explosion, but the props were gone, and the roof had come down from end to end, for all he knew.

"Is there no other way out?" said Carthew.

"None, sir."

Carthew indicated the row of openings beside them.

"Don't any of these lead anywhere?"

"They all lead to the main road, except that one at the end, which leads to the intake. We have plenty of room to move about, and plenty of air; but we are shut in, and that's a fact, sir."

"Is that your opinion too, Mr Wilkie?"

"We canna get gettin' oot o' this, sir," replied the oracle with complacent finality.

There was a deathlike silence. Then Master Hopper began to cry softly. He was going to die, he reflected between his sobs, and he was very young to do so. It was hard luck his being there at all. He had only joined the riot from youthful exuberance and a desire to be "in the hearse," as an old Scottish lady once bitterly observed of a too pushful mourner at her husband's funeral. He entertained no personal animosity against the owner of the pit: in fact he had never set eyes on him. His desire had merely been to see the fun. Well, he was seeing it. He wept afresh.

Atkinson and Denton sat and gazed helplessly at Carthew. The part they had played in sealing up six souls in the bowels of the earth had faded from their minds: to be just, it had faded from the minds of their companions as well. The past lay buried with Renwick and Davies. The future occupied their entire attention.

There was another danger to be considered—the suffocating after-damp of the explosion. Carthew inquired about this. Entwistle considered that the risk was comparatively slight.

"The cloths hung across the approaches to the main road should keep it away," he said. "It's a heavy gas, and don't move about much, like. We shall be able to tell by the lamps, anyway."

"Then what had we better do?" said Carthew briskly. "Dig?"

One of the men—Atkinson—lifted his head from his hands.

"Ah were saaved by t' Salvationists once," he said hoarsely. "Ah could put up a prayer."

"I think we will try the effect of a little spade-work first," said Carthew. "*Laborare est orare*, just now!" he added to himself.

A few hours later they re-assembled. They had tapped, sounded, hewed, and shovelled at every potential avenue of escape, but to no purpose. The intake and main road appeared to be blocked from end to end. Six men were mewed up with no food, a very little water, twenty-four hours' light, and a limited quantity of oxygen; and they had no means of knowing how near or how far away help might be.

All they were certain of was that on the other side of the barrier which shut them in men were working furiously to reach them in time, and that up above women were praying to God that He would deliver them.

CHAPTER TWENTY.

BLACK SUNDAY.

The search party had concluded its investigations, and stood at the foot of the shaft, which fortunately had not been injured by the distant explosion, waiting for the cage.

A pit-bottom is an unexpectedly spacious place, more resembling the cellars of a ducal mansion, or a city station in the days of the old under-ground, than a burrow in the hidden places of the earth. Whitewashed brick archways open up long vistas, illuminated by electric lamps. Through an adjacent doorway streams the cheerful glow of the engine-room, from which the haulage of the trucks is controlled. Only in the "sump," below the level of the flooring at the foot of the shaft, the water gleams black and dismally.

"Is there any other road to explore, Mr Walker?" asked a huge man in blue overalls, with a patent breathing apparatus strapped upon his back.

"No, Sir John. All we can do at present is to get the ventilating gear going again, and then send down a double shift to get to work on the main road, in the hope of finding some one alive at the end of it. Meanwhile we will go up and look at the pit-plan."

"How long do you think it will take to get through? You know more of the geography of this pit than I do."

"It depends on how far the roof is down. It will be slow work, for we must re-prop as we go. Twenty yards an hour is about the best we can expect to do, working top-notch all the time. And if the road is blocked from end to end, as well it may be, it will be a question of days, Sir John."

"And in Number Three they have neither food nor drink?"

"Neither, to our knowledge. Probably they have a little water, though. We must get at them double quick. Here is the cage coming down."

The cage roared upwards between the wooden guides, black with long use and glistening with oil and water; and presently the party were back in the great shed which covered the pit-head, pushing their way through anxious inquirers to the office buildings.

Leaving the other members of the search party—an overman and two hewers—to report progress, Sir John and his manager shut themselves into the inner office. Here Walker unrolled the pit-plan, which, with its blocks and junctions and crossings, looked very like an ordinary street map.

"Here we are," he said. "We have been able to explore the whole pit except this part here"—he dug the point of his pencil into a distant corner—"and the reason is that the means of access to that particular level are blocked. Here is where the block begins." The pencil swiftly shaded in a section. "There is the intake, all blown to smithereens; that and the road to Number Three. But if there are men alive in the pit, Number Three is where we shall find them."

"Do you believe that they are alive?" asked Juggernaut.

"I do. It seems incredible that the whole roof should have come down. We must get the ventilating plant in order and dig them out; that's the only way. We should be able to start work immediately."

"Right!" said Juggernaut, bracing himself at the blessed thought of action once more. "I'll call for volunteers."

A minute later, appearing at a brilliantly lit window, he addressed the silent throng below him. To most of them this was the second speech that they had received from him in twelve hours.

"We have been down the pit," he said. "There has been a biggish explosion, and Number Three is cut off by a heavy fall. The air below will be breathable in less than an hour, and we are going to set to work right away, and clear, and clear, and clear until we find out whether there is any one left alive there. Now,"—his voice rang out in sudden and irresistible appeal—"we want *men*, and plenty of them. Short shifts and high pressure! Those poor fellows have very little water, no food, and a doubtful air supply. I ask for volunteers. Who will come down? Step forward—now!"

A gentle ripple passed over the sea of upturned faces. Then it died away. The distance between the speaker and his entire audience had diminished by one pace.

"Thank you!" said Juggernaut simply. "I knew I had only to ask. Mr Walker, will you call the overmen together and get going as soon as possible?"

A few hours earlier the men of Belton had failed in an enterprise for lack of a leader. Now they had found one.

———

Sir John Carr drove the first shovel into the mass which blocked the main road, and for the space of thirty minutes he set a standard of pace in the work of rescue which younger and more supple successors found it hard to maintain.

Shift followed shift.

Sunday morning dawned up above, and the sun swung into a cloudless April sky, but still the work below went on—grim, untiring, unprofitable work. Hope deferred succeeded to hope deferred.

Twenty-four hours of blind energy advanced the rescuers three or four hundred yards, but there seemed to be no end to the fall. Progress was growing slower too, for the excavated material had to be carried back farther every time. Once during the second night word was sent up the shaft that two men had been hurt through a fresh fall in the roof, over-eagerness being the cause. Still the work went on. And so Black Sunday drew to a close, to be succeeded by a Monday of a very similar hue.

CHAPTER TWENTY-ONE.

VEILLESSE SAIT.

Lady Carr was at the pit-head early on Monday morning. She had arrived in the Belton motor, just in time to provide for the conveyance of the two injured men to the county hospital, eleven miles away. She herself passed quietly in and out amid the anxious groups of men and women. She said little: it was not a time for words; but it was noted that she lingered for more than a few minutes in the company of Master Hopper's mother, and that her grave, slow smile appeared to hearten that broken widow mightily.

Presently she encountered her husband, whom she had not seen for two nights and a day.

"You here?" he said.

"Yes. I have sent those two poor men away to Kilchester in the car, and I am waiting for it to come back." Then a note of maternal severity intervened. "Have you been to bed at all since I last saw you?"

"Not much," admitted Juggernaut. "But I have a vague recollection of lying down somewhere for a few hours last night. It may have been on the office sofa or it may have been in the sump. What I am more certain of is that I have not washed for days. I feel like Othello. But what has brought you down to the pit?"

"I thought you would like to know," said Daphne, "that this affair is in the morning papers."

Othello looked, if possible, blacker than before.

"Have they got the names?"

"Yes, Jim Carthew's too. And what do you think the result has been, Jack? I have had a wire from—from—" for a moment Daphne's concern for the tragedy around her was swallowed up in the joy of the match-making sex over one sinner that repenteth—"whom do you think?"

"I don't know."

Daphne told him. "It was the first thing she heard when she landed in England. She is *frantic* about him, and is coming down here to-day. She has offered to sleep anywhere, do anything, if only she may come. Jack, isn't it too heavenly?" Daphne positively crowed.

Juggernaut's teeth flashed across his grimy countenance in a sympathetic smile.

"You women!" he said softly. "We must fish him out for her after this, Daphne. Well, Mrs Entwistle?"

A middle-aged woman with hungry eyes was at his elbow. She was Amos Entwistle's wife.

"Would you come and speak to old Mr Entwistle, sir?" she said—"my man's father. He is too rheumatic to move about easy, but he seems to have something on his mind about another way of getting at them."

Sir John Carr turned and followed her promptly.

"Shall I come too, dear?" said Daphne.

"Better not. Go and send Walker to me if you can find him."

Mrs Entwistle conducted Juggernaut to a sunny nook, sheltered from the keen breeze, against the brickwork of the power-house. Here sat Entwistle senior, stone-deaf, almost blind, but with his eighty-year-old wits still bright and birdlike.

He was no respecter of titles or employers, this old gentleman, and in high-pitched, senile tones he criticised the arrangements for rescue. The excavatory operations were a mistake. Time was being wasted. The poor lads inside had nobbut a little water to drink and nowt to eat. The air would be getting foul, too.

"You must get there *quick*, Sir John," he said, rising painfully from his seat. "See now."

He began to hobble laboriously away from the vicinity of the pit-head towards the rather grimy fields which lay to the north of the colliery. By this time Walker had arrived, bringing with him a burly, bearded pit-inspector, sent down by the Board of Trade.

Twenty minutes' laborious walking ended in a halt in the middle of a bleak pasture-field, from which a few unconcerned sheep were extracting some exceedingly dubious-looking nourishment. Mr Entwistle called a halt.

"Been thinking things over," said he, breathing stertorously. "Known this country-side, above and below, nigh seventy year. The lads, they go buzzing round the pit-head, but the old man"—as a matter of fact he said "t'owd mon," but it will be simpler to paraphrase his utterance—"sits at home and thinks things over. They has to come to him in the end!"

All this was highly irrelevant and proportionately exasperating; but old age has its privileges. Doubtless Agamemnon, Menelaus, and other eager stalwarts longed with all their hearts to tear Nestor limb from limb, what time that venerable bore delivered himself of fifty lines of autobiographical hexameters as a preliminary to coming to the point; yet they never did. Presently Mr Entwistle concluded his exordium and tapped upon the ground with his staff.

"We are standing," he announced, "right over the road to Number Three. Two hundred fathom down," he added, in case they should have overlooked this point.

This, at anyrate, was a statement of fact. Walker produced and consulted the pit-plan. "You are about right," he said. "Well?"

"How far along this road is the face?" inquired the old gentleman. "It's a tidy number of years since I——"

Walker told him, with the result that the excursion was resumed. Presently Mr Entwistle came to a halt again.

"We're over Number Three now," he said.

Walker again confirmed him, with the aid of a compass-bearing and the pit-plan.

"Well?" he said.

The old man pointed with his stick to some dismantled and abandoned pit buildings farther down the valley, a full mile away.

"The old Shawcliffe Pit," he croaked. "Worked out this forty year. But I knowed it well when I were a lad."

Juggernaut, suddenly seeing light, caught the old man by the arm.

"You mean," said he rapidly, "that the Shawcliffe workings run up this way——"

"No, no," said Walker, interrupting. "You are wrong, Mr Entwistle. The Shawcliffe workings all run down the other way, to the north."

"Nay," persisted the old gentleman—"not all. They thowt there were a seam this way, and they drove one road out here, if so be they might pick it up. They had got signs of it, boring. But it were a faulty seam. It weren't until Belton Pit were opened, thirty years later, that they struck it fair."

"And that road runs out this way, from Shawcliffe shaft?" asked the Inspector.

"Ay, and it must come very nigh to the Belton Workings now—nigh to Number Three. I reckon——"

"He is right!" said Walker excitedly. "It's a chance! I *have* heard of this road, now I think of it." He turned to Entwistle again. "How far out do you think it runs? Quick, man—tell us!"

For answer the veteran, much inflated, stumped off again in a northerly direction, with all the assurance of a water-diviner in full cry. After fifty yards or so he stopped.

"I should say it ended about here," he said. "You can trust the old man's memory. The youngsters——"

Another lengthy deliverance was plainly threatened, but this time our Nestor observed, not without justifiable chagrin, that the majority of his audience had disappeared. The symposium was suddenly reduced to himself and his daughter-in-law.

Testily curtailing his peroration, to the exclusion of severable valuable aphorisms upon the advantages of senile decay over youthful immaturity, the old gentleman resignedly took the arm of Mrs Amos, and permitted himself to be conducted back to his fireside.

But he had served his turn for all that.

The other three were hurrying back to Belton Pit talking eagerly, Juggernaut leading by half a pace.

"It's madness, of course," said Walker cheerfully. "This pit has been closed for forty years. The props will be down——"

"The air will be foul," said the Inspector thoughtfully.

"Or explosive," added Walker.

"And there will probably be water," continued both together.

"Is the shaft still open?" asked Juggernaut brusquely.

"I believe so," said Walker.

"I suppose it would be possible to rig a derrick and tackle over it?"

"Yes."

They strode on a dozen paces.

"I am going down," said Juggernaut.

"I am going with you," said Walker.

"And I," said the Inspector, "am coming too."

They broke into a trot.

CHAPTER TWENTY-TWO.

HOLD THE FORT!

The safety-lamps had burned themselves out hours ago, and the imprisoned party sat on in the dark. There was nothing else to do. Food they had none: their water was exhausted. They slept fitfully, but in the black darkness sleep seemed little removed from death, and time from eternity.

Jim Carthew lay with his head upon a friendly lump of coal, pondering with his accustomed detachment upon the sundry and manifold changes of this world. He thought of Death. Plainly he and his companions were about to solve the mystery of what lay hidden round that corner which our omniscience is pleased to consider the end of all things. What would they find there? Another life—a vista more glorious and sublime than man in his present state could conceive? Or just another long lane—just another highway of labour and love, of service and reward? Or—a *cul-de-sac*—an abyss—a jumping-off place? He wondered. Not the last alternative, he thought: more likely one of the other two. Anyhow, he would know soon, and it would be interesting. His one regret was that he would not be able to come back, even for five minutes, to tell his friends about it.

Friends!...

This brought a new train of reflection. He thought of Jack Carr and Jack Carr's wife. Would the latter keep her promise, and come back to her husband? He wondered. She should be in Belton this week, all being well— that is, if this was the week he thought it was. But time seemed rather a jumbled affair at present. Besides, he was so infernally hungry that he could not reason things out. Never mind!...

He thought of Nina Tallentyre. *That* difficulty had solved itself, anyhow. No need for further hopings or strivings: that was a relief! When their rupture occurred he had prayed to be excused from living further. He had even petitioned that the earth might open and swallow him up for ever. Well, the earth had done so, so he ought to be satisfied. He was gone down into silence, and Nina was rid of him—well rid of him! He was well rid of her, too. She had led him a dog's life the last few months. A *dog's* life. He repeated the fact to himself pertinaciously, but without any great feeling either of conviction or resentment.

He felt strangely contented and cheerful. His mind dwelt with persistence on the bright side of things. He thought of the day when she and he had first met, and Nina, in her superb, imperious manner, had desired him to take her out of "this rabble," and come and amuse her in a corner. He remembered subsequent meetings; various gracious acts of condescension on Nina's part; and finally one special evening on board a yacht in regatta-time, when they had sat together in a corner of the upper deck in the lee of the chart-house, with a perfectly preposterous moon egging them on, and the faint strains of *Caressante* pulsing across the silent water from the Commodore's yacht hard by; and Nina had nearly—almost—all-but—and then actually—capitulated.

She had gone back on her word three weeks later, it was true; but he drew consolation even now from the memory of something which had slipped through her long lashes and rolled down her cheek even as she dismissed him, a memory which had carried through many a black hour.

It was over episodes like this that his mind lingered. Other and less satisfactory items declined to come up for review. Perhaps, he reflected, dying men, provided they had lived clean and run straight, were always accorded this privilege. Only the credit side of the ledger accompanied them on their journey into the unknown. It was a comforting thought.

...He wondered what she would think when she heard about it. In a blue envelope at the bottom of his private strong-box they would find his will, a primitive document composed in secrecy, and endorsed: "To be opened when I have gone out for good." In this he had bequeathed all he possessed to "my friend Miss Nina Tallentyre," be she maid, wife, or widow at the moment. Carthew was not a man who loved by halves. All that he had was hers, whether she needed it or not. Of course she must not be made conspicuous in the matter; he had seen to that. The bequest was to be quite quiet and unostentatious. No probate, or notices in the papers, or rot of that kind. In the blue envelope was enclosed a private letter to his lawyers, dwelling on the importance of this point. They were decent old buffers, that firm, and would understand. They would square up any death-duties and other legal fakements that were necessary, and then pass on the balance to little Nina, to buy herself pretty things with. But no publicity! No embarrassment!

...He fell asleep, and dreamed, from the natural perversity of things, of roast beef and Yorkshire pudding.

When he awoke, low voices were conversing near him. Farther away he could hear the regular breathing of Master Hopper, who, with youth's ready amenability to Nature's own anodynes, was slumbering peacefully.

"I can weel understand, Mr Entwistle," observed Mr Wilkie in measured tones, "that no decent body would like to be seen entering yin o' they Episcopalian Kirks."

Amos Entwistle's heavy voice agreed. He commented with heat upon indulgence in vain repetitions and other heathen practices favoured by the Anglican community; and related with grim relish an anecdote of how his own daughter, lured from the Wesleyan fold by the external fascinations of the new curate, had once privily attended morning service at the parish church—to return, shocked to the foundations of her being, with horrific tales of candles burning on the altar in broad daylight and the Lord's Prayer repeated four times in the course of a single service.

"But what I couldna thole," continued Mr Wilkie, who had been characteristically pursuing his own line of thought in the meantime, "would be no tae belong tae the kirk of the *land*. A Chapel body! I could never endure the disgrace of it."

Entwistle demurred vigorously. It was no disgrace to be Chapel folks. Sturdy Independents were proud to be able to dispense with State-aided, spoon-fed religion. Disgrace, indeed! Were not Mr Wilkie's qualms on the subject of Dissent due rather to a hankering after the flesh-pots—the loaves and fishes—the——

"Well, perhaps no exactly a disgrace," continued Mr Wilkie, disregarding the latter innuendo, "but a kin' o' stigma, like. Man, it's an awful thing tae walk doon the street and meet the minister o' the pairish, and him pass by and tak' no more notice of ye than if ye were a Plymouth Brother or an Original Secessionist. I mind yince when I was in a Tynside pit, I sat under Mr Maconochie—him that gave up a grand kirk in Paisley tae tak a call tae oor wee bit Presbyterian contraption, Jarrow way. Now, although Mr Maconochie's kirk was my kirk and him oor minister, I used tae feel far more uplifted if I got a good-day frae the minister o' the English Kirk— Golightly, or some sic' name—an *Episcopalian*! I canna imagine why, but there it was. I doot it was just orthodoxy. He was the minister o' the kirk o' the land, and Mr Maconochie, being, for him, on the wrong side of the Border, was not. Gin I had met yon felly Golightly trapesing doon the High Street o' Jedburgh, things would hae been gey different; for then——"

The point at issue, Entwistle's deep patient voice asseverated, was this. Should a man who was an Independent allow himself or his bairns to have aught to do with Church folk on any pretence whatever?

He was answered in the darkness by a third voice. Denton, the hewer— Atkinson, the retired Salvationist, shovelled and wheeled away in a tub what Denton hewed—had awoken from an uneasy sleep, and was listening to the conversation. Of all that little band, probably he was the least prepared to die. He was a drunkard, a blasphemer, and an evil liver. But like the rest of us, he had his redeeming features. He had inspired and kept alive for a period of ten years the love of his wife—a feat which many an ex-sidesman, buried beneath a mountain of expensive masonry adorned by an epitaph beginning, "Well done, good and faithful servant!" has signally failed to accomplish. He sat up now.

"Ah niver 'ad nowt to do wi' churches or chapels," he began defiantly. "But ah knaws this. When my Maggie were lyin' badly four years agone, and us thought she was goin' to die, she asked me to go and fetch her pastor—dash;that's what she called him. Ah ran along to his house and begged him to come. He said"—the man's voice grew thick, and one could almost see his sombre eyes glow in the gross darkness—"he said he were busy! There was a swarry that neet that 'twas his duty to attend, and next day he was goin' off to a political meeting to protest against t' Education Bill, or summat. He said, too, that he had enough to do ministerin' to the wants o' them that deserved ministerin' to, wi'out comin' to the house o' the likes o' me. When had he last seen me in t' chapel, he would like to knaw? Yes, *that* was what he wanted to knaw! He wanted to stand and ask me questions like that when my Maggie——!... Ah cursed him, and his chapel, and his fat-bellied deacons till Ah were out o' puff with it: then Ah went off down the street half-crazed. There Ah runs straight into a young feller wi' a soft black hat and long legs. He was standing outside t' door of his lodgings, smoking a pipe in the dark. He was t' curate at t' parish church, and when he saw I wasn't in liquor, he asked me what was my trouble. I telled him. 'Is that all?' says he. 'Will I do? I've just come off my day's work, and I ain't got nothing to do but amuse myself now.' It were nigh ten o'clock. Well, he comes with me, and he sat by my Maggie all the neet through, and sent me with a note to a doctor that were a friend of his, and only went away himsel' at seven o'clock next morning, because he had to get shaved and take early service or summat. *That's* all your chapel folk ever done for me, Amos Entwistle."

"That was a special case, and proves no rules. Besides," said Entwistle soberly, "this is no time for religious differences. We are in God's hands now, and I doubt we shall all be in a place soon where there is neither Church nor Chapel."

"Would it no be best for us all tae keep silence for a matter o' ten minutes," suggested Wilkie, "and pit up a bit prayer each of his ain, we bein' no all of the same way of thinkin' in these matters? That gate, wi' so many prayers o' different denominations goin' up, yin at least should get gettin' through the roof of the pit. Are ye agreed, chaps?"

"Ay, ay!" said Entwistle.

The others all murmured assent, save Master Hopper, who shrieked out in sudden fear. The proximity of death had become instantly and dreadfully apparent to him on Mr Wilkie's suggestion. Carthew reached out and pulled him to his side.

"Come over here, by me," he said.

Master Hopper, greatly soothed, crept close, and settled down contentedly enough with an arm round Carthew's shoulders. Presently Carthew heard him repeating The Lord's Prayer to himself in a low and respectful whisper.

The silence lasted longer than ten minutes. For one thing, the supplicants were exhausted in body, soul, and spirit, and their orisons came slowly. For another, there was no need to hurry. For nearly an hour no one spoke.

At length some one sat up in the darkness, and the voice of Atkinson inquired—

"Mr Carthew, sir, I think a song of praise would hearten us all."

"I believe it would," said Carthew. He was not enamoured of the corybantic hymnology of the Salvation Army, but the horror of black darkness was beginning to eat into his soul, and he knew that the others were probably in a worse plight. "What shall we sing?"

"At the meeting where I were saved," said Atkinson deferentially, "we concluded worship by singing a hymn I have never forgotten since: *Hold the Fort!*"

"That sounds a good one," said Carthew, struggling with an unreasonable sensation of being in the chair at a smoking-concert. "Does any one else here know *Hold the Fort?*"

Yes, Entwistle knew it. Master Hopper had heard it. Mr Wilkie had not. He did not hold with hymns: even paraphrases were not, in his opinion, altogether free from the taint of Popery. If it had been one of the Psalms of David, now! Still, he would join. Denton knew no hymns, but was willing to be instructed in this one.

Atkinson, trembling with gratification, slowly rehearsed the words, the others repeating them after him.

"We will sing it now," he said.

He raised the tune in a clear tenor. Most north-countrymen are musicians by instinct. In a few moments this grim prison was flooded by a wave of sonorous melody. The simple, vulgar, taking tune swelled up; the brave homely words rang out, putting new heart into every one. Each and all joyfully realised that there are worse ways of going to one's death than singing a battle-song composed by Moody and Sankey. With drawn white faces upturned to the heaven they could not see they sang on, flinging glorious defiance into the very teeth of Death—gentleman and pitman, Church and Chapel, zealot and infidel.

"Last verse again!" commanded Atkinson.

"Wait a moment!" cried Entwistle, starting up.

But no one heard him. The chorus was rolling out once more—

"*Hold the Fort, for I am coming——*"

Tap, tap, tap! Scrape, scrape, scrape! Hammer, hammer, hammer!

The hymn paused, wavered, and stopped dead on the final shout.

"By God!" screamed a voice—it was Denton's—"here they are!"

Carthew, with Hopper's arms tightening convulsively round him, started up.

"Is it true?" he asked hoarsely.

"Ay! Listen! They have found us. They are within a few yards of us," said Entwistle.

"*Praise God, from whom all blessings flow!*" sang Atkinson suddenly and exultantly, and the others joined him.

Entwistle was right. They were found. Reasoned calculation, dogged persistence, and blind indifference to their own safety had brought the search party triumphantly along the mouldering rickety passages of Shawcliffe Pit to the nearest point of contact with Number Three in Belton; and *Hold the Fort!* proceeding from a subterranean cave of harmony not many yards away, had done the rest.

CHAPTER TWENTY-THREE.

THE LAST TO LEAVE.

It was night once more, and the great arc lights snapped and sizzled above the waste-heaps and truck-lines surrounding the head of Belton Pit. But the scene was deserted. The centre of interest had shifted to Shawcliffe, a mile away. Here a vast silent throng of human beings stood expectantly in groups, their faces illuminated by the naphtha flares which had been erected here and there about the long-abandoned pithead.

There was news—tense, thrilling news—and the prospect of more. The ancient shaft had been opened and a bucket and tackle rigged—there was no time to ship a cage—and a search party had gone down at dusk. Word had shortly been sent up that the road to the south was still open, though the air was foul and the props rickety. Then came a frantic tug at the rope, and a messenger was hauled to the surface, crying aloud that men were alive in Belton Pit. It was hoped, he added, that the search party would reach them by midnight, for the dividing wall was surprisingly thin. Sir John Carr's order was that blankets and stretchers should be prepared; also food and medical comforts, for the prisoners had fasted for something like sixty hours. With that the messenger had dived below once more, and the game of patience was resumed.

It was past midnight now, and everything was in readiness. On the outskirts of the throng, at the side of the rough and lumpy road, stood a motor-car with two occupants—women. One of them was her ladyship; the other the spectators failed to recognise. But there were rumours about to the effect that she was a visitor to Belton recently arrived from London. Lady Carr had been seen meeting her at the station that afternoon.

The stranger's name, had it been told, would not have conveyed much information to the watchers. It was Nina Tallentyre.

There was a sudden swirl and heave in the crowd. The hand-turned windlass was at work again, and some one was being hauled slowly up the shaft. It was Mr Walker, the manager.

They made a lane for him, until he reached a convenient rostrum formed by an inverted and rusty truck. This he mounted and very briefly told them the news—news which made them laugh foolishly and sob by turns. There was no cheering: they were past that.

In the excitement the next man who followed him up the shaft passed unnoticed. It was Sir John Carr. He saw the hooded motor standing apart, Mr Vick sitting motionless at the wheel. Next moment he was in beside the two women, overalls and all, holding Daphne's hands in a single grimy fist and telling them what we know already.

"Is he *perfectly* safe?" asked Nina for the tenth time. She did not possess Daphne's aristocratic composure under critical circumstances.

"Yes—but very weak. I am sending him up second. The first is a pit-boy. When Carthew arrives you had better put him in the motor and take him straight home."

"Jack!" said Daphne.

She slipped out of the car and accompanied her husband into the darkness outside the radius of flaring lights.

"Are you going down again?" she asked.

"I am."

"And when are you coming up?" The unflinching courage which upholds so many women in the face of danger had never failed Daphne during those long days and nights. But now the courage was receding with the danger.

Juggernaut smiled.

"When would you have me come up?" he asked.

"Last," said Daphne, suddenly proud. "It is the only place for you. I will wait here. Nina can take her Jim home, and the car can come back later for you and me. Jack!"

Her husband turned and regarded her curiously. Their eyes met.

"Well?" he said.

"Jack," continued Daphne in a low voice, "is there much risk down there— for you, I mean?"

"There is always risk, of a sort, down a coal-pit," replied her husband pontifically. "A little explosive marsh-gas, or a handful of finely divided coal-dust lying in a cranny, might suddenly assert itself. Still, there are risks everywhere. One might be struck down by apoplexy at a vestry meeting."

Daphne gave his arm a squeeze, an ingratiating childish squeeze, suggestive of the Daphne of old negotiating for extension of dress allowance.

"Jack, stay up here! You have done enough."

"*Post me, Satanella!*" smiled her husband. Then, more seriously: "Daphne, if I came to you and asked for orders *now*, where would you send me, I being what I am—the proprietor of the pit—and you being what you are—the proprietress of my good name?"

Daphne's fit had passed.

"I should send you," she answered bravely, "down the shaft, with orders to stay there until every one else was safely out."

"I obey," said Juggernaut. "*Au revoir!*"

"Jack!" said Daphne faintly. Her face was uplifted.

"It will be a coaly one!" said her husband, complying. Then came an accusation.

"Daphne, you are trembling! This is not up to your usual standard."

"I can't help it," said Daphne miserably. "I am a coward. But I don't mind," she added more cheerfully, "so long as no one else knows. *You* won't give me away!"

At that Juggernaut held her to him a moment longer.

"Daphne, my wife," he whispered suddenly—"thank God for you—at last!"

Then they fell apart, and she ran lightly back to the motor and Nina.

Once she turned and looked over her shoulder, waving her hand prettily. Her face, framed in a motor bonnet and lit by the glare of a naphtha light, looked absurdly round and childish, just as it had done upon a dim and distant morning in Snayling Church.

It was the last time in his life that her man was ever to behold it.

Master Hopper, partially restored by brandy and meat juice, and feeling, on the whole, something of a hero, arrived at the pit-head an hour later, there to be claimed by his mother and hustled off, by more willing hands than he could comfortably accommodate, home to bed. The bucket, which provided standing-room for two passengers, then went down again.

This time it brought up Mr Walker, holding a supporting arm round Carthew—a sick man indeed. He was less hardened to subterranean existence than the rest. Sympathetic murmurs arose. The bucket was swung out from beneath the pulley and landed gently on the edge of the shaft. Carthew stepped out and stood swaying uncertainly.

A tall girl came suddenly forward.

"Jim, dear!" was all she said.

Carthew surveyed her, and smiled weakly.

"Hallo, Nina! That you?"

Miss Tallentyre took his arm.

"The car is waiting for you," she said. "Lean on me *hard*, old boy!"

And certainly no more desirable prop than this girl, with her splendid youth and glorious vitality, was ever offered to a weary mortal. Carthew, dazed but utterly content, put a feeble arm round the slim shoulders of the woman whose mere hand he had hitherto counted it heaven to touch, and the pair passed away together out of the crowd—and out of this narrative. Happiness has no history.

Others were coming up the shaft now. First Mr Wilkie, in a very fair state of preservation: then Denton, the reprobate, insensible—his hands were in tatters, so fiercely had he worked,—then Atkinson, still sheer drunk with the success of his own hymnology: then Amos Entwistle.

Denton's huge inanimate form was laid on a stretcher, to be carried home under the direction of his wife. (The wives of Renwick and Davis, poor souls, had gone home long ago.) But, the Belton Hall motor returning on that instant, Lady Carr insisted on carrying husband and wife home together. The rush through the night air brought Denton round, and he was able to walk into his own house, leaning undeservedly upon the proudest little woman in the north of England.

Daphne returned to the pit-head for the last time. The rescue work was completed. Surely she might claim him now!

No, the block and tackle were not working. No one else was coming up at present. Only round the shaft a knot of men conferred eagerly. She would wait in the car.

She lay back, wrapped in a rug—a cold dawn was breaking—and closed her eyes. The rush and excitement of the three days had told upon her. She had no clear recollection of having slept for any length of time or eaten at any definite period. She had done work among stricken wives and mothers that Belton village would never forget, but she had not realised this. All her head and heart were filled by the mighty knowledge that after five years of married life she and her husband had found one another.

Meanwhile there was silence round the pit-head.

"Vick," said Daphne, suddenly fearful, "go and find Mr Walker, or some one, and ask when Sir John will be up."

Mr Vick, who had been dozing comfortably at his wheel, clambered down into the muddy road and departed as bidden. Ten minutes later he returned falteringly.

"Mr Walker has just gone down the pit again, my lady," he said. "There has been a slight explosion of coal-dust, I was to tell you. Nothing serious— just a flash and a spit in a holler place in the roof, the message said."

"Is Sir John down there?" Cold fear gripped Daphne's heart.

"Yes, my lady."

"Is he safe, do you know?"

"I couldn't say, my lady," replied Vick doggedly. "I'll inquire."

He turned away, glad to escape, with the brisk demeanour of one anxious to investigate matters. But before he reached the pit-head the answer to all possible inquiries came to meet him, in the form of a slow-moving procession carrying something in its midst.

Very gently the bearers laid the stretcher on the grass by the roadside. Daphne, white, silent, but composed, stooped down and turned back the blanket which covered her husband's face. He lay very still. His head and eyes were roughly bandaged. Daphne whispered, so low that none other could hear.

"Jack—my Jack!"

His voice answered hers, from amid the bandages—faint, but imperturbable as ever.

"I'm all right, dear. Afraid it has got me in the eyes a bit, though. Take me home, wife of mine! You will have to lead me about with a string now!"

Daphne's head sank lower still, and she whispered, almost exultantly--

"At last I can really be of some use to you!"

CHAPTER TWENTY-FOUR.

ANOTHER ALIAS.

"Brian Vereker Carr," inquires a voice, "what time is it?"

"Half-past four, sir," replies the same voice respectfully. "In twenty minutes"—in a more truculent tone—"you will have to go upstairs and get ready for tea. You will have to wash your hands—and your face too, I expect," adds the voice bitterly.

Thus, at the age of eight, does Master Brian Vereker Carr commune with himself—a habit acquired during an infancy spent in a large nursery where there was no one else to talk to. The necessity for this form of duologue no longer exists, for now a sister shares the nursery with him—Brian lives in dread of the day when she shall discover that her manly brother not only owned but once rejoiced in the great doll's house in the corner by the fireplace—but the habit remains. Besides, Miss Carr is only four years old, and gentlemen who have worn knickerbockers for years find it difficult to unbend towards their extreme juniors to any great extent. Hence Mr Brian still confers aloofly with himself, even in the presence of adults. There are touches of Uncle Anthony Cuthbert about Brian.

At present he is inadequately filling a large arm-chair in front of the library fire at Belton. The fire is the sole illuminant of the room. The curtains are closely drawn, for it is a cold winter evening. Brian Vereker continues his observations, now approaching an artistic climax.

"If you go upstairs promptly *and* obediently, like a good boy, what do you think mother will give you?" inquires voice number one.

"Chocolates!" replies number two, with an inflection of tone which implies that it will be playing the game pretty low down if mother does not.

The owner of both voices then turns an appealing pair of brown eyes upon Daphne, who is sitting on the other side of the fireplace, engaged in the task of amusing her four-year-old daughter.

"We'll see," she replies after the immemorial practice of mothers.... "And suddenly," she continues to the impatient auditor on her lap, "his furry skin fell away, and his great teeth disappeared, and he stood up there straight and beautiful, in shining armour. He *was* a fairy prince, after all! Brian, dear, tumble out of that arm-chair. Here is dad."

Daphne must have quick ears, for a full half-minute elapses before the door opens and a figure appears in the dim light at the end of the room. Apparently the darkness does not trouble him, for he circumnavigates a round table and a revolving bookcase without hesitation, and finally drops into the arm-chair recently vacated by his son.

"Brian Vereker Carr," inquires a small and respectful voice at his elbow, "do you think dad will play with you to-night?"

"I am *sure* he will," comes a confident reply from the same quarter, "if you give him two minutes to light his pipe in, and refrain from unseemly demon—demonstrations of affection in the meanwhile."

"It's a hard world for parents," grumbles Juggernaut, getting up. "Where is my tobacco-pouch?"

His hand falls upon the corner of the mantelpiece, but encounters nothing there but a framed photograph of a sun-burned young man on a polo-pony—Uncle Ally, to be precise.

"Now where on *earth* is that pouch? I know I left it on the left-hand end of the mantelpiece after lunch."

There is a shriek of delight at this from Brian, in which Miss Carr joins, for the great daily joke of the Carr family is now being enacted.

"Where can it be?" wails Juggernaut. "Under the hearthrug, perhaps? No, not there! In the blotting-pad? No, not there! *I* know! I expect it is behind the coal-box."

Surprising as it may appear, his surmise proves to be correct; and the triumphant discovery of the missing property scores a dramatic success which no repetition seems able to stale. (This is about the fiftieth night of the run of the piece.)

Presently the pipe is filled and lit, Master Carr being permitted to kindle the match and Miss Carr to blow it out, the latter feat only being accomplished by much expenditure of breath and a surreptitious puff from behind her shoulder, contributed by an agency unknown.

"Now, Brian, young fellow," announces Juggernaut, "I will play for ten minutes. Let me speak to the sister first, though."

He lifts his daughter, whom he has never seen, from her mother's knee, and exchanges a few whole-hearted confidences with her upon the subject of her recreations, conduct, dolls, health, and outlook on life in general. Then he restores her, and shouts—

"Come on, Brian Boroo!"

There is a responsive shriek from his son, and the game begins. It is not every boy, Master Brian proudly reflects as he crawls on all fours beneath a writing-table, who can play at blind man's buff with a real blind man!

Daphne leans back in her chair and surveys her male belongings restfully. Time was when this husband of hers, at present eluding obstacles with uncanny facility and listening intently, with the youthful zest of a boy-scout, for the excited breathing of his quarry, found life a less hilarious business. There rises before her the picture of a man led from room to room, steered round corners, dressed like a child, fed like a baby—shattered, groping, gaunt, but pathetically and doggedly cheerful. Neither Daphne nor her husband ever speak of that time now. Not that she regrets it: woman-like, she sometimes feels sorry it is over and gone. She was of real use to her man in those days. Now he seems to be growing independent of her again. Then she smiles comfortably, for she knows that all fears on that score are groundless. He is hers, body and soul. And she——

A small, unclean, and insistent hand is tugging at her skirt, and Miss Carr, swaying unsteadily beneath the burden of a bulky and tattered volume, claims her attention.

"Show me pictures," she commands.

She and her tome are hoisted up, and the exposition begins.

"Where did you find this book, Beloved?" inquires Daphne. The book is an ancient copy of the 'Pilgrim's Progress,' and we have encountered it once before in this narrative.

"Over there," replies Beloved, indicating the bottom shelf of a bookcase with a pudgy thumb—"under ze 'Gwaphics.' What's ze name of that genelman?"

To Miss Carr distinctions of caste are as yet unknown. In her eyes every member of the opposite sex, from the alien who calls on Thursdays with a hurdy-gurdy to the knight-in-armour who keeps eternal vigil in the outer hall, is a "genelman." Even if you are emitting flames from your stomach, as in the present instance, you are not debarred from the title.

Daphne surveys the picture in a reminiscent fashion, and her thoughts go back to a distant Sunday morning at the Rectory, with her youngest brother kneeling on the floor, endeavouring to verify a pictorial reference in this very volume.

"What is he doin' to the other genelman?" continues the searcher after knowledge upon her knee, in a concerned voice.

"He is trying to hurt him, dear."

"What for?"

So the inexorable, immemorial catechism goes on, to be answered with infinite patience and surprising resource. Presently the cycle of inquiry completes itself, and the original question crops out once more.

"What did you say was ze name of that genelman?" with a puckered, frowning effort at remembrance.

"Apollyon, dear."

"Oh." Then the inquirer strikes a fresh note.

"Do you know him?"

"I used to," replies Daphne. "At least," she adds, "I used to know some one who I thought was like him. But his name turned out not to be Apollyon after all."

"What *was* his name, then—his pwoper name?" pursues Miss Carr, deeply intrigued.

Daphne turns to another illustration, coming much later in the book, and surveys it with shining eyes.

"His proper name, Beloved?" she asks.

"Yes. What *was* it?"

"Mr Greatheart," says Daphne softly.

THE END.